conscious CHOICES

A MODEL FOR SELF-DIRECTED LEARNING

Elaine Gray, Ph.D.
ROLLINS COLLEGE

SHARON AINSLEY
CONTRIBUTING AUTHOR

PEARSON
Prentice
Hall

Upper Saddle River, New Jersey
Columbus, Ohio

Library of Congress Cataloging-in-Publication Data

Gray, Elaine.
    Conscious choices : a model for self-directed learning / Elaine Gray.
        p.   cm.
    Includes bibliographical references and index.
    ISBN 0-13-112931-7
    1. Self-culture—Handbooks, manuals, etc.   2. Continuing education—Handbooks,
manuals, etc. I. Title.

LC32.G74 2004
371.39'43—dc21
                                      2003054908

Vice President and Executive Publisher: Jeffery W. Johnston
Senior Acquisitions Editor: Sande Johnson
Assistant Editor: Cecilia Johnson
Editorial Assistant: Erin Anderson
Production Editor: Holcomb Hathaway
Design Coordinator: Diane C. Lorenzo
Cover Designer: Jeff Vanik
Cover Image: Robert Johnson
Production Manager: Susan Hannahs
Director of Marketing: Ann Castel Davis
Director of Advertising: Kevin Flanagan
Marketing Manager: Christina Quadhamer
Compositor: Aerocraft Charter Art Service
Cover Printer: Coral Graphic Services
Printer/Binder: R. R. Donnelley & Sons Company

Pearson Education Ltd.
Pearson Education Singapore Pte. Ltd.
Pearson Education Canada, Ltd.
Pearson Education–Japan

Pearson Education Australia Pty. Limited
Pearson Education North Asia Ltd.
Pearson Educación de Mexico, S.A. de C.V.
Pearson Education Malaysia Pte. Ltd.

10 9 8 7 6 5 4 3 2 1
ISBN 0-13-112931-7

Contents

Chapter 2

CHOICES: CRITICAL THINKING   25

Chapter 3

ATTENTION: COMPREHENSION AND FOCUS   49

Chapter 4
ENERGY: MENTAL AND PHYSICAL WELL-BEING   75

Chapter 5

EMOTIONAL INTELLIGENCE: SELF-MASTERY   93

Chapter 6

INTEGRITY: MOTIVATION AND ACCOUNTABILITY   113

Chapter 7

INTEGRATION: TIME AND LEARNING   129

Acknowledgments

This book would not have been possible without the significant contributions of my colleagues, mentors, and the editorial staff at Prentice Hall. First, I extend my deepest gratitude and admiration to Sharon Ainsley, who not only wrote the Student Perspectives and offered suggestions on the material, but who supported me through the process by sharing so much of her enthusiasm, time, and life energy. Sharon is a shining light and brilliant scholar whose stories should stir those who read them into reaching their potential as successful students. Without her interest and input, this book would not have made it past the outline stage.

I want to thank Mrs. Eve Walden, who was the Director of Student Success Programs at Valencia Community College in the mid-1990s, for suggesting to me that I should consider teaching a student success course. Though I had never imagined myself in the role of a college instructor, with her guidance and encouragement I embarked on a new career. I am also indebted to author Dave Ellis for originally giving me the tools and inspiration to teach and to write about student success.

I extend my gratitude to my colleagues, Dr. Pat Fox and Karen Stonebridge, who early on worked with me as a team and provided the creative impetus and ideas for designing Web-based curricula for student success courses.

Cecilia Johnson and Sande Johnson from the Prentice Hall editorial staff provided me with high-quality assistance and feedback. My thanks go to them for believing in my ideas and helping me take them to the next level.

Others who provided invaluable feedback and suggestions include the reviewers: Alicia Andujo, Long Beach City College; Barbara S. Doyle, Arkansas State University; Marianne Fitzpatrick, Bauder College; Cindra Kamphoff, University of North Carolina Greensboro; Patsy Krech, University of Memphis; Judith J. Pula, Frostburg State University; Kim Smokowski, Bergen Community College; David A. Young, Cerritos College; and Beatrice Zamora-Aguilar, Southwestern College. Their comments and critiques served to make this book more cohesive and accessible.

Finally, I wish to acknowledge my parents, John and Mary Ruth Gray, for making my higher education possible and for always supporting me in my creative endeavors.

In my own quest to become a lifelong, self-directed learner, I am grateful for all of the teachers who brought richness and openness to my life. I dedicate this book to the mother of my consciousness, Mrs. Emma Ourbanak.

About the Authors

Elaine Gray, Ph.D.

Elaine taught student success courses in the classroom and on-line at Valencia Community College from 1995 to 2001. During this time, she was nominated for *Who's Who in American Teachers*. She holds a Masters in Liberal Studies from Rollins College and has completed postgraduate work in learning theory at Florida State University. Her Ph.D. from the California Institute of Integral Studies focused on learning and change in human systems. The topic of her dissertation research centered on the study of emotional intelligence in on-line student success courses.

She has worked with publishers as an author, trainer, and developer of Web-based student success curricula. She has an extensive background in multimedia design and audio/video production. Elaine appears as a keynote speaker at student success conferences throughout the country.

Elaine's teaching strategies are influenced by social constructivism as well as active and collaborative learning. She uses dialog and self-reflection as primary teaching tools. In her own studies, she learned firsthand the value of peer-to-peer learning as a method to widen and deepen perspectives. Her emphasis on case studies and reflective inquiry derives from the belief that a student's experiential involvement creates lasting and meaningful learning experiences. This book is grounded in exercises designed to help students become self-directed learners with principle-driven goals. Elaine believes that through conscious choices students can create success and prosperity in life.

Dr. Gray currently teaches at Rollins College in Winter Park, FL.

Sharon Ainsley, *Contributing Author, Student Perspectives*

Sharon brings her experience as a college student to the book through writing the Student Perspectives and by providing ideas for the chapter case studies and summary materials.

Sharon began working with Elaine Gray in 1999 as a teaching assistant for an on-line student success course. While performing the roles of wife, mother of three children, full-time college student, and member of the workforce, she learned ways to integrate her choices and balance the values of

her life with the demands of the college environment. She believed so profoundly in the value of self-directed learning that she worked for over three years as a student mentor, using her personal experience to help fellow students make similar learning connections for themselves.

Sharon has earned a number of academic distinctions, including the Ellen Knowles Harcourt Foundation Award, the National Communications Foundation Scholarship, National Dean's List recognition, and Who's Who in American Junior Colleges awards. She was recently awarded the prestigious Barry Goldwater Scholarship for the 2003–2004 school year. She is currently a computer science major who plans to teach at the university level and conduct research in learning implementations for computer-based artificial intelligence technology in the areas of distance education and learning disabilities. Sharon earned her associate's degree with honors from Valencia Community College. She remains at the top of her class while pursuing her degree at Rollins College in Winter Park, FL.

She dedicates her work here to her husband, Richard, for all his love, support, and inspiration—and to her children, Bastian, Heather, and Monica.

Companion Website

DISCOVER THE COMPANION WEBSITE ACCOMPANYING THIS BOOK

The Prentice Hall Companion Website: A Virtual Learning Environment

Technology is a constantly growing and changing aspect of our field that is creating a need for content and resources. To address this emerging need, Prentice Hall has developed an online learning environment for students and professors alike—Companion Websites—to support our textbooks.

In creating a Companion Website, our goal is to build on and enhance what the textbook already offers. For this reason, the content for each user-friendly website is organized by chapter and provides the professor and student with a variety of meaningful resources.

For the Professor—

Every Companion Website integrates **Syllabus Manager**™, an online syllabus creation and management utility.

- **Syllabus Manager**™ provides you, the instructor, with an easy, step-by-step process to create and revise syllabi, with direct links into Companion Website and other online content without having to learn HTML.
- Students may log on to your syllabus during any study session. All they need to know is the web address for the Companion Website and the password you've assigned to your syllabus.
- After you have created a syllabus using **Syllabus Manager**™, students may enter the syllabus for their course section from any point in the Companion Website.
- Clicking on a date, the student is shown the list of activities for the assignment. The activities for each assignment are linked directly to actual content, saving time for students.

- Adding assignments consists of clicking on the desired due date, then filling in the details of the assignment—name of the assignment, instructions, and whether or not it is a one-time or repeating assignment.
- In addition, links to other activities can be created easily. If the activity is online, a URL can be entered in the space provided, and it will be linked automatically in the final syllabus.
- Your completed syllabus is hosted on our servers, allowing convenient updates from any computer on the Internet. Changes you make to your syllabus are immediately available to your students at their next logon.

For the Student—

- **Chapter Objectives**—Outline key concepts from the text.
- **On-line Journal and Demonstration of Competency**—These competency centered activities encourage students to directly apply and articulate their understanding of chapter topics. After students complete the activity, they are given the option to send their response to up to four email addresses (professor, teaching assistant, study partner, etc.).
- **Web Destinations**—Links to www sites that relate to chapter content.
- **Message Board**—Virtual bulletin board to post or respond to questions or comments from a national audience.

To take advantage of the many available resources, please visit the *Conscious Choices: A Model for Self-Directed Learning* Companion Website at

www.prenhall.com/gray

Introduction

Our lives are a sum total of the choices we have made.

—WAYNE DYER

WHY SHOULD I USE THIS BOOK?

This book is based on the idea that to get more from life, you must become more. To be more means mastering your attitudes and behaviors in order to direct your learning experiences and achieve the outcomes you desire.

Higher education introduced the concept of lifelong learning because it is expected that the average person will change careers several times during his or her life. *Knowing how to learn has become the ultimate foundational skill that supports success on all levels and in all situations.* Students, employees, and even consumers must be able to learn and adapt to rapidly changing situations and technologies. You are also expected to learn and adapt to the responsibilities of your changing roles in life, as you become parents, peers, colleagues, or life partners. If you can learn quickly from your mistakes, you avoid unnecessary or prolonged suffering. Most importantly, if you can connect your values and goals with your moment-to-moment choices, you will move toward balance, integration, and well-being in all aspects of your life.

Conscious Choices approaches learning from the inside out. Instead of first looking at those techniques and methods that students can use to increase memorization and study skills, *this textbook helps learners become self-directed through developing an emotional readiness to learn.*

HOW IS THE BOOK ORGANIZED?

Conscious Choices teaches students how to use critical thinking and self-awareness to clarify goals, focus attention, and sustain energy. Students are taught four core competencies: critical thinking, comprehension, motivation, and self-mastery. Each competency area has a student success skill set that is essential to becoming a self-directed and emotionally intelligent learner. The student success skill sets were selected to meet the expectations and demands of higher education. The four competency areas and their skill sets are:

CRITICAL THINKING

- Know the source of personal influences
- Account for personal assumptions and the assumptions of others when distinguishing fact from opinion
- Consider multiple perspectives
- Question, reassess, and be open-minded
- Handle problem solving

COMPREHENSION

- Sustain a prolonged focus
- Listen actively with less distractions
- Observe details accurately and objectively
- Remember information
- Apply what is learned to real-life or abstract situations (e.g., tests)

MOTIVATION

- Clarify personal values
- Articulate goals
- Prioritize expenditures of time and energy
- Become self-motivated
- Manage procrastination and distractions

SELF-MASTERY

- Develop a self-awareness
- Become self-responsible
- Be confident
- Be health conscious
- Become adaptable

WHAT IS COMPETENCY-BASED LEARNING?

This textbook does not use memorization as a method of assessing student skills or understanding. There are no multiple-choice or true–false quizzes associated with this textbook. Instead, journal exercises, case studies, and demonstrations of competency help you consider, discuss, and discover how to apply what you are learning to real life.

Journaling provides you opportunities to informally practice your writing skills while exploring your thoughts, feelings, or ideas. Writing about your thoughts can help you develop a sense of clarity. Once you have completed a journal exercise, you will be better prepared to participate in class discussions on the topics you write about. When you see the Companion Website (CW) icon, it means the journal exercise is also available on the Prentice Hall Companion Website. Your instructor will let you know if you should submit your journal by e-mail or on paper.

The *Try This* exercises are designed to encourage your experiential participation in the chapter concepts. In some ways, this method is more difficult than studying for a test because you must *show what you know* both by your actions and your thoughts. For example, participating in classroom discussions will be an important measure of your competency because it shows you have contemplated the topics. Competency-centered learning requires students to make use of their knowledge by sharing it in discussions. The *Case Studies* are designed as group critical-thinking exercises to share your perspectives with your classmates.

This book requires that you actually do something and apply your learning to real-life situations. Because the measure of personal growth or inner change is subjective, each chapter concludes with a *Demonstration of Competency* exercise that allows you to apply the chapter concepts to your immediate life situations. Reaching a state of competency means that the concepts expressed in these pages are *mastered through the experience of living them* in a variety of real-life and abstract situations. Your competency with the text's concepts is demonstrated by your ability to speak or write in detail about how you have or will apply them.

THE CHAPTERS

Conscious Choices teaches you how to use critical thinking and self-awareness to clarify your values and goals during the decision-making process. The first two chapters, *Self-Directed Learning* and *Choices*, help you understand *how to make informed, intentional, and integrated choices.* By understanding how your values and decision-making skills are developed, you can learn how to direct your choices to reach the goals you desire.

The next two chapters, *Attention* and *Energy,* deal with how to develop and maintain a focused and receptive state. *Your ability to focus attention, sustain energy, and manage well-being is vital to comprehension.* Knowing how to maintain attention is a key factor in being successful while taking tests, employing memorization skills, and listening actively.

Instead of looking strictly at the classic step-by-step techniques to improve study skills, the book looks at your *individual character* or aspects of *self-mastery* that must be developed and fine-tuned for you to become a better learner. Chapter 5, *Emotional Intelligence,* and Chapter 6, *Integrity,* show that qualities such as self-awareness and self-motivation are directly related to leadership and success in college and life. Emotional intelligence includes positive attitudes, optimism, and appropriate responses to challenging or difficult situations and people.

The final chapter, *Integration,* looks at the direct connection between time and integrity. *How you choose to spend your time* is the ultimate test of your skill and will.

Before beginning Chapter 1, take a few minutes to complete the Pre-Assessment on the following pages. The assessment is designed to give you a snapshot of your strengths and weaknesses in the four core competency areas. At the end of Chapter 7, you will have an opportunity to reassess yourself to see how you have improved.

HOW SHOULD I READ THIS BOOK?

The chapters of this book can be read in any order. It is recommended that you read all of the chapters and complete all of the exercises. Your instructor may find it useful to have certain sections of the book read out loud, and then ask you to discuss some of the exercises you completed based on the readings. This book was written with classroom discussions in mind. Many of the ideas are theoretical and open to multiple perspectives. Talking about your interpretations of or your experiences with the concepts in the book is key to developing a meaningful understanding of how these ideas can bring about extraordinary success in life and college. You can also discuss the text's ideas with friends and coworkers. Talking about the ideas prepares you to apply the concepts in life. You should read the book *actively,* keeping these questions in mind:

How can I apply this idea to my life?

Is this statement true for me? Why or why not?

What other examples can I think of that this concept applies to?

Why could this be valuable to me as a college student?

Who can I talk to about this concept to help me understand it better?

Asking questions and verifying for yourself the usefulness of the ideas is a first step in making conscious choices.

Pre-Assessment

Instructions: Rate yourself on the following student success skill sets.

STUDENT SUCCESS SKILLS	RATING
Rating Scale *1 = I am a star 2 = I could do better 3 = I need major improvement*	
CRITICAL THINKING	
Before I make decisions, I consider how various factors will influence my choices.	
I frequently examine the source of my beliefs and opinions to determine their ongoing validity.	
I can respect and acknowledge beliefs and opinions that are different from or conflict with my own.	
I am not afraid to ask questions or request assistance.	
I am open to learning new things and willing to find different ways to do things.	
Total Points	
MOTIVATION	
I clearly understand my personal values.	
I prioritize my time and energy based on my personal goals.	
I am not afraid to take the initiative.	
I am aware of the primary source of my motivation.	
I know how to minimize procrastination.	
Total Points	
COMPREHENSION	
I know how to sustain my focus and concentrate on what I am doing.	
I am in control of my responses to inner and outer distractions.	
I observe details accurately.	
I can remember information and concepts.	
I can apply what I learn to real-life or abstract situations.	
Total Points	

SELF-MASTERY	
I am mindful of my actions and my thoughts are self-reflective.	
I am trustworthy and accountable for my words and actions.	
I have good self-esteem.	
I practice healthy living through my choices of what I take into my body and senses.	
I am flexible, resilient, and adaptable to change in my life or living environment.	
Total Points	

Record the total points for each core competency:

Critical Thinking = _____ (max 15)   Comprehension = _____ (max 15)

Motivation   = _____ (max 15)   Self-Mastery   = _____ (max 15)

Grand total for all competencies = _____ (max 60 points/min 20 points)

For comparison purposes, you will take this assessment again after you finish reading the book.

Self-Directed Learning

VALUES AND GOALS

We don't receive wisdom; we must discover it for ourselves after a journey that no one can take for us or spare us.

—MARCEL PROUST (1871–1922)

S elf-directed learning is structured around the goal of becoming a learner who approaches life and education with intention, integrity, and enthusiasm. The skill of being self-directed is developed with a clever combination of knowledge and practice. Self-directed learners understand the relevance of values and goals in their learning and decision-making processes. By examining the source of your values, you will see how these influences impact your moment-to-moment choices. This critical-thinking process provides you with an opportunity to affirm or modify your beliefs and direct your goals and learning experiences accordingly. Self-directed learning empowers you to take full responsibility for the quality of your education.

What If . . .

What if learning something new was the only source of entertainment in your life? What might be the first subject you would indulge in?

CHARACTERISTICS OF A SELF-DIRECTED LEARNER

Self-directed learners have the skills necessary to make learning an interesting and rewarding experience. They take a leadership role in their educational process and are identified by their passion and persistence when it comes to tackling new or difficult material. They care enough about their education to be involved and participate on a variety of levels, from making time to meet with their instructors to supplementing their learning through additional research. They are focused on learning what they have to know to meet their personal goals, and they maintain positive, open states of mind. Self-directed learners make learning meaningful by seeing the relationship between their education and their aspirations. The key characteristic of self-directed learners is their ability to take full responsibility for the quality of their learning experiences.

Passion for Learning

An emotion that motivates a sense of learner responsibility and creates a desire for active involvement is a simple love of learning. Learners who can generate a love of learning and passionately move toward their goals are not dependent on any grading system or program requirements for their success. Their motivation is internalized and is directly related to meeting their desired goals. The sustained power of a positive emotion such as love, excitement, or hope can balance the difficult or demanding aspects of college life.

Your ability to learn is shaped by what you feel and how much you value the learning process. Whether or not you view learning as important or meaningful creates most of the inner attitudes and aptitudes that you bring to your learning experiences. How you value your educational opportunities affects your ability to comprehend and apply your lessons. Generating your own excitement about learning gives you the energy, resilience, and determination to overcome obstacles. By becoming a self-directed learner, you can operate independently of external reward systems—you are rewarded by your own experience of learning.

If you do not value the educational process, you should question why you are attempting the rigors of college life. Maybe this sounds like a hard line, but self-directed learning presumes you are learning because you want to. No person, situation, or institution can make you learn—you must take ownership of your learning.

One of the greatest barriers to learning is a basic lack of interest. Many college students are just not clear on why they are attending. They do not have a specific degree or career goal in mind, and they do not have any enthusiasm for the classes they take. If you take classes only because they are required, your aptitude for learning is seriously diminished.

Try This

FEELINGS ABOUT LEARNING

Take a moment to evaluate how you feel about learning something new.

1. Describe several of the *emotions* that occur when you are working toward learning and mastering new material.

2. Describe any learning situations that bring positive emotions and make you feel good.

3. Write a paragraph that explains why you do or do not care about your education.

4. How do negative emotions affect your ability to learn?

Self-directed learning means you are self-motivated and hungry for a meaningful learning experience. When you are deeply interested in a topic, you can enhance the instruction offered by teaching yourself the material. When you are following this principle, it keeps you moving along in a state of high interest and curiosity—you don't wait for an instructor to tell you how or why the lessons are important. If the instructor or the materials are not providing you with the quality of engagement you prefer, then you find creative ways of supplementing your learning experience. Self-directed learners are actively involved in deepening their own learning process.

Student Perspective

SELF-RESPONSIBILITY

A good example of how **active involvement** applies to the college experience is class participation. You know the story—out of the 30 people in your class, there are usually 4 or 5 students who are always asking questions, offering answers, going up to the board, or reading out loud from the textbook. These people just seem to have all of the answers and have no problem showing it—they act like the whole class is centered around them! Well, guess what? It usually is. Although this type of behavior may seem like "showing off," or being a "know-it-all," these students are demonstrating

exactly what self-directed learning is all about! They have chosen to embrace their classroom experience to the fullest and are not content to sit and just listen. They are engaged with the material, interested in knowing more, actively interacting with their teacher and peers, and seeking new insights. They have decided to get every penny's worth of their tuition money. They have chosen to get all they can out of the college experience. Usually, they are the students who get the best grades—not because they annoyed the rest of the class with all of their chatter, but because they have taken responsibility for their own learning experience and become active participants in it. That is what it is all about.

REFLECTION QUESTIONS

1. Do you consider yourself a student who participates actively in class? Explain why. Discuss whether or not you feel your level of involvement is sufficient. If not, how can you improve it?

2. How does taking personal responsibility for the learning process relate to your ability to retain and apply information and concepts?

Receptive States of Mind

An old Zen saying is: "When the student is ready, the teacher will appear." Learners can be given the tools and materials, but they cannot be made to learn. Students are taught study skills, told about their learning styles, and given memorization techniques, yet rarely do their learning experiences carry a lasting impression. This is the frequent frustration of many extremely skilled teachers. Usually, students are not taught how to open up to the learning process. Being receptive means knowing how to generate the energy necessary to relax and focus your attention. To remember what was learned, you must first receive the information in an open state of mind. Teachers cannot make you learn. They can only facilitate your learning process. Ultimately, it is you, the student, who must mentally prepare to arrive at the learning experience in an open and willing state.

Self-directed learning requires that you develop and practice a highly receptive state. Developing a quiet and empty mind is often thought of as a technique reserved for martial arts masters or sports professionals. This is not a skill that students are accustomed to fine-tuning. To absorb and comprehend the volumes of written and spoken material you will be exposed to in the college environment, you must walk into class each day with a mind that is prepared. Self-directed learning makes the learner responsible for reaching this degree of self-mastery.

Receptivity begins when you stop thinking and your inner dialog stops talking. You begin to listen actively when you are able to create an empty and open mind. This may sound contradictory, but experiment with the following exercise and see if you can notice a difference in your ability to be receptive.

Try This

SCRIPTING INNER DIALOG

Sometimes, you do not notice the inner dialog that goes on while you are trying to listen to someone talk. If your mind is busy critiquing or carrying on its own conversation, you do not really hear or remember what is said.

Step One.   This exercise works best if read out loud by two people. Have one person read the directions (in capital letters) while you read the inner dialog part (in italics). In this exercise, you are going to intentionally script your inner dialog while listening to someone give directions.

> TO GET TO THE TOWN MALL, TAKE HIGHWAY 20 FOR EIGHT MILES. *I have to remember to return that birthday gift. I really would rather have the money and go shop at another store.* TAKE EXIT 17. *Highway 20 is such a pain, it has been under construction for six years! I would rather take Highway 8 and come back toward town from the west!* GO EAST ABOUT SEVEN MILES. *This is a bad time of day for traffic. Maybe I should stop at the mall on a Monday morning when it will not be so busy.* YOU WILL PASS THE POLICE STATION. *Oh my, I forgot to pay that parking ticket! I hope there is not an extra fee!* THEN TURN RIGHT. *Boy am I hungry.* MAKE ANOTHER RIGHT AT THE FIRST LIGHT. *I think I know a better way to get there than this.* THEN LEFT AT THE SECOND STREET. *I doubt these directions are correct. I think it is a left at the third street.* THE MALL IS EIGHT MILES DOWN ON YOUR LEFT.

Step Two.   Immediately close your book and write down what you remember of the directions.

Step Three.   Try reading a new set of directions, but this time script your inner dialog to do what is called subvocalization. When you subvocalize, you keep your inner dialog quiet by echoing what the speaker is saying in your mind. Again, the directions are in capital letters and your inner dialog script is in italics. After you have finished the reading, close your book and write down what you remember of the directions.

TO GET TO THE STADIUM, TAKE HIGHWAY 40 TO EXIT 27. *Highway 40 to exit 27.* TAKE A LEFT TOWARD DOWNTOWN AND GO ABOUT TWO MILES. *Left to downtown, two miles.* GO RIGHT AT THE THIRD LIGHT AND THEN LEFT AT THE SECOND LIGHT. *Third light right, second light left.* GO ANOTHER FOUR MILES TO 7TH STREET AND TAKE A LEFT. *Four miles to 7th Street and left.* THE STADIUM IS ON THE RIGHT.

Step Four. Describe how you experienced the two different inner dialogs. Why might one inner dialog method be more helpful than the other?

What If . . .

What if colleges did not have pre-designed majors or programs of study? What if they allowed learners to set their own learning objectives and follow their own enthusiasm? What program of study would you design for yourself? What would be the topics in the courses?

Purpose and Direction

Required courses guide students through a program of study. Unfortunately, some of this course work may have little personal meaning. College programs or degrees have required courses that relate to the needs of business and industry or are prerequisites for higher degrees. Grades are generally competitive, and instructional strategies are usually based on students learning what is necessary to earn a specific letter grade or score. So, students *learn to earn.* Grades, jobs, and a graduation date serve as the primary motivators. Some students just do the minimum required to earn a grade. In this situation, the learning process quickly becomes empty and meaningless. Many students only do what is necessary to get through college and miss the opportunity to understand the wider implications and applications of the subjects they study. The college degree means nothing more than "been there, done that."

Most students rely on the research and vision of their colleges or universities to connect the dots necessary to prepare them for rewarding careers. Those educational institutions that have moved in the direction of student-designed majors have discovered that most students are unprepared to set their own academic goals upon entering college. Because about 80 percent of freshmen and many sophomores have "undecided" majors, many students' careers are determined by the classes they take or the subjects they are most successful in.

Self-directed learning asks you to understand *why you are learning* before you can create a learning experience. What you learn has little value or meaning beyond a test date if you do not understand why you are learning in the first place. Knowing what you want to achieve and setting goals helps you focus your motivation and turn what you are learning into a lasting impression. When you can *learn what you must know* in order to achieve what you want, you are satisfying a basic life purpose.

Self-directed learners tend to make the best use of all of the opportunities an educational system has to offer. After deciding on their academic and career goals, they take the courses and use the college resources necessary to accomplish them. They make their program of study meaningful by keeping their personal values and goals in mind.

IDENTIFYING THE SOURCES OF YOUR VALUES

Values are powerful invisible influences that affect the way you think, feel, judge, and compare. They determine what is meaningful to you. Self-directed learning requires that you articulate and understand your personal values. When you can articulate your values, you are able to make informed choices and act with integrity. Without an awareness of your values, other influences can gain the upper hand and control how you spend your time and energy. In the absence of clear personal values, you might choose activities that are detrimental to your health or well-being. A classic example of the absence of clear values for college students occurs when they are influenced to spend time on activities that negatively impact their grades.

Values can be highly situational and are redefined with time and experience. Throughout your life, you will re-evaluate the values and principles you live by, keeping the ones that are sacred and discarding those that no longer seem appropriate. Most importantly, you must choose which values and principles to transmit to your children and to affirm with your peers.

For Your Journal

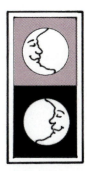

VALUES EXPLORATION

*Please respond to the following in your journal or by using the **Journal Module** on the CW.*

An important question to ask is *who or what taught me my values?* Typically, you will find the root of your values in the following sources:

Parents

Religion

Peers

Media such as TV and movies

Educational institutions or teachers

Life experiences

In the first part of this exercise, you are asked to rate which sources have influenced your values on *personal health.* For example, think about the values you hold about nutrition, personal hygiene, fitness, and vitality. Note what pictures, voices, or memories come up when you think of the ideal weight or body strength. Do you select your food based on taste or a diet you've read about? Usually, you will find a *combination of influences,* some of them not so obvious. To accurately complete this exercise, set aside about 20 minutes to truly reflect on who or what informs your beliefs and ideals. Take time to dig deep and attempt to reveal all of the influences you can remember for each category, and then rate them from the highest to the lowest range of influence.

1 = very little to none   2 = not much   3 = some   4 = considerable   5 = primary

Personal Health

VALUE INFLUENCERS	RATING
Parents	
Culture	
Religion	
Peers and friends	
Media such as TV, films, and magazines	
Educational institutions or teachers	
Life experiences	

Use the same rating system to evaluate how your values related to *education* have been shaped.

1 = very little to none   2 = not much   3 = some   4 = considerable   5 = primary

Education

VALUE INFLUENCERS	RATING
Parents	
Culture	
Religion	
Peers and friends	
Media such as TV, films, and magazines	
Educational institutions or teachers	
Life experiences	

Now, use the system to rate how your values regarding *money* were shaped.

1 = very little to none   2 = not much   3 = some   4 = considerable   5 = primary

Money

VALUE INFLUENCERS	RATING
Parents	
Culture	
Religion	
Peers and friends	
Media such as TV, films, and magazines	
Educational institutions or teachers	
Life experiences	

Now that you have rated the influences in these three areas, what are the primary sources of your values overall?

VALUES AND CRITICAL THINKING

Values inform your opinions and your opinions shape your decisions. The values that guide your decisions regarding health, education, and finance have probably been influenced by several sources. Reviewing what you rate as the primary sources of your values teaches you something about what and who you value. For example, if your highest rated influence is consistently TV and movies, then you can safely assume that you value the media as an authority over the other influences listed in the exercise.

You may also note that you occasionally do not know the original sources of your values. Values can be subconsciously ingrained in you by complex emotional and mental impressions over time. You start to see your values in action when you criticize or compliment others. Your values are continuously revealed in your choices.

If you cannot trace the roots of your values, you may find yourself in situations where you are unable to make sound decisions or take steps toward aligning your choices with a desired outcome or personal goals. In your educational experiences, a lack of awareness of your values can contribute to distractions that adversely affect your grades. When you lose touch with your values, your decisions can be controlled by people who prefer that you not think for yourself. Advertisers are delighted when they can control your values—they stand to gain plenty of money and recognition when the masses value one brand name over another. Politicians and newscasters also are professionally trained "influencers." To create an opinion that is truly your own, you must be able to practice critical thinking and look beyond the authority of commercial advertisers or the manipulations of media figures. First and foremost, this requires that you are constantly in touch with your own values. Reaffirming or articulating your values is key to making conscious choices.

FIGURE 1.1   Values in action.

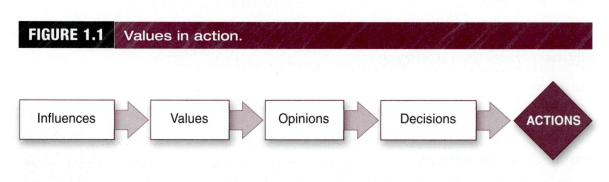

Core Values

Core values are basic and universal—they typically transcend culture, upbringing, media, and peers. The ultimate core value, which the majority of the human race instinctively shares, is the value of life. There are innumerable value subsets that can be connected to the valuation of life. Your individual perspectives and belief systems inform and support these core value subsets. *Try asking yourself if each of your daily decisions is made with an awareness of how you value life.* Not just your life, but all life. Asking this question repeatedly throughout the day or week will reveal to you the threads of your personal core values.

Situational Values

Values and belief systems are learned. You may, however, occasionally find yourself in a hypocritical situation—you say you have certain values, but due to a life situation, you act in a manner that does not represent your beliefs. For example, you may be a law-abiding person and pride yourself on being honorable. This value becomes situational when you decide to download music and movies off a pirate Internet site. Another example of situational values might be if you, for ethical reasons, are a vegetarian, but when having dinner with your partner's parents for the first time, you eat some of the chicken casserole so you do not offend the cook.

Your values can be flexible and adaptable and still be reliable sources of guidance for your personal lifestyle. The process of defining your values is not a one-time decision that you are locked into. With life experiences and knowledge, you can expect that your values and accompanying beliefs will grow and change. A huge part of your educational experience will be based on understanding and respecting a wide variety of cultures, philosophies, and belief systems.

Student Perspective

ADAPTABILITY AND OPEN-MINDEDNESS

Open dialog requires open-mindedness. Each of us has been raised in our own faith system and has some idea of our political standing. Sitting in a classroom and listening to a professor talk about things that you do not believe in or agree with can be a difficult experience and make learning almost impossible. The topics and ideas presented as factual can sometimes be in direct opposition to your own ideas and beliefs. Worse yet, you will most likely be tested on the material later!

The important thing to keep in mind is that you do not have to abandon your own beliefs and principles in order to learn about or accept those that are different. Values are adaptable, and for a student in one of these difficult situations, it is vital to understand that the experience is a learning process—not a reconditioning exercise. No one expects you to blindly and suddenly adopt these beliefs or ideas as your own. Everyone views the world and life differently. The learning process asks that you be open-minded enough to understand new ideas and learn about beliefs that may be radically different from your own. In short, you are expected to manage multiple perspectives. If something you learn changes your perspective or makes you question the validity of what you hold as "true," it is a wonderful opportunity for growth and self-exploration. This does not make your original ideas invalid or wrong; rather, it can help to build, affirm, and expand upon them; redirect them; or augment them in a way that reflects new wisdom. The values or principles that emerge from such growth can be very positive influences in your life. By remaining receptive despite an initial discomfort, you afford yourself the opportunity for continued growth and new understandings.

REFLECTION QUESTIONS

1. When you are confronted with views that are radically opposed to your own, how do you handle the situation?
2. Being able to argue both sides of an opinion is considered a sign of mastery in critical-thinking skills. Can you think of an example of an opinion you hold where you could make a strong case for either side?

Not *My* Values

People typically adjust and redefine their values over time based on what they observe and experience. As you examine how sources and situations shape your values, it is equally as important to acknowledge when you have rejected certain value systems. You may live your life reacting to the values of your parents, peers, or religion. As you grow up observing how your parents make choices, you sometimes decide to rebel against what you perceive to be the values they hold. This value system rejection still expresses your values.

An error in critical thinking occurs when you rebel against a value system yet remain unclear about the values you will adopt to replace them.

Sometimes, this gap in values allows other unconscious and occasionally negative influences to manipulate you by default. For example, you may reject the value held by your parents that says you should invest and save money for your future. Without a replacement value, you may find that, as an adult, you do not know how to handle your money profitably. A word of caution, before you reject a value, take care that you have clarified a worthy replacement.

What If . . .

What if a government committee dictated your career goals? Can you see how freedom and planning might go hand in hand?

PLANS AND GOALS

The first and probably the only necessary step in planning is to know what you want to accomplish in life. Common sense says that when you know what you want, you can make your time and efforts more productive to those ends.

Begin your planning by formulating specific goals. For example:

"I plan to complete this year of college with a 3.5 GPA or better."

"I plan to spend more time nurturing my two dogs."

"I plan to increase my physical strength, and I plan to get a better paying job."

Plans are much like goals. Stating your goals as something you will do and making a plan to do it in a specific amount of time not only helps you remember what's important, it is also the first step toward becoming accountable. When you identify your goals and state them as a plan, you are more likely to speak about your goals with other people. Talking about your goals can sometimes bring immediate results. Words are very powerful door openers. For example, many job interviewers will ask you to discuss your career objectives or goals. Individuals who can speak about how their goals relate to their future role in the company are often viewed more favorably or are seen as better candidates for those jobs that require leadership skills. Talking about your goals also lets people know you aspire to improve upon your best. This in itself is an admirable reflection on your character.

For Your Journal

STATING YOUR GOALS

*Please respond to the following in your journal or by using the **Journal Module** on the CW.*

This journal activity asks that you reflect on your life goals in three areas and indicate what you will do to accomplish them over time. Indicate each goal in the space provided, then complete the sentences that follow. Give careful thought to this, but don't be afraid to dream big!

ACADEMIC GOAL

In three years, I will

In one year, I will

In one month, I will

This week, I will

Today, I will

CAREER GOAL

In three years, I will

In one year, I will

In one month, I will

This week, I will

Today, I will

PERSONAL GOAL

In three years, I will

In one year, I will

In one month, I will

This week, I will

Today, I will

Try This

MATCHING GOALS AND VALUES WITH CHOICES

Making conscious choices requires that you know your goals and values and apply them to your day-to-day, moment-to-moment decisions. Ideally, you should constantly check your choices to ensure that they align with your long-term aim. Use this process for the coming day to see if you can match your goals and values with your choices.

Instructions: Note the decisions and choices you make today—from the mundane to the momentous. Your choices can be as simple as whether to eat a certain type of food, who you speak to and what you say, or which clothes you decide to wear. More complex decisions, such as who to vote for or how to invest money, may have multiple goals and values in play. Use the table below to capture at least five decisions you make in a typical day. Then, articulate the personal goal and values that supported and informed each decision.

Describe the decisions or choices you made today.	Indicate the goal that informed this decision.	What are the values that informed the decision?
I chose to attend the seminar on health care benefits.	My goal to maintain my health using preventative medicine.	I value the quality of life and my well-being.

The purpose of this exercise is to get you thinking about the importance of making conscious choices and decisions based on your own values and goals—thinking for yourself instead of following the status quo.

FIGURE 1.2 Values in decision making.

Values → Reflections → Emotions → Goals → **DECISIONS**

Practicing Conscious Choices

One method of practicing the conscious decision-making process is to frequently ask yourself whether your decision will serve your personal values and goals or whether it will contradict them in some way. Many times, you can actually sense when there is a contradiction of your value system. You might notice it as physical discomfort, stress, or confusion. For example, if you make a choice to take a telemarketing job that you suspect is misleading customers, you may feel additional anxiety or irritability while working. Over time, you can learn to turn off these signals, or you may actually change your values to match the current situation. You turn off your value of honesty by telling yourself something like, "I am not really lying to them. If they are dumb enough to believe me, then that's their problem!" Another example of how values can become "situational"—you may believe in the value of honesty, but while working for the telemarketing company, you disregard that value and give a higher priority to the money you can earn.

Being in alignment with your personal values and goals may not be possible all of the time. However, a *simple moment of reflection* prior to making a decision creates the possibility that alignment will occur. Individuals actually begin to be mindful of their values when they stop to consider them.

Student Perspective

COMMUNICATING VALUES

Your personal values determine the direction you want your future to take, and the college environment is often the first step toward creating that future. You cannot, however, start building a future on a shaky foundation! Imagine, if you will, a college freshman in a big state university. She has a full scholarship and has been placed in advanced courses based on her entrance scores. She is all set for success, right? Well—not necessarily. If she has clearly determined her own set of personal values and is acting in alignment with those values in order to achieve her goals, then YES—she will excel and be very successful. The exact opposite is true if she has not identified or clarified her personal values. If she is confused as to what she really wants out of life, what kind of work she wants to do, and where she wants to end up, she may find herself feeling stuck, hopeless, and unhappy. Her attitude will likely reflect her discomfort, her grades may suffer, and she might find herself shifting majors every year or even dropping out entirely just so she can feel less trapped. How can she feel confident and successful if she doesn't even know what it is she wants to succeed at or why? How can she travel the road to success if she has not yet articulated to herself what her goals and values really are?

The truth is some amount of uncertainty or apprehension is normal and healthy; we are all a little ambiguous about what we want in life, and that is OK. There are so many opportunities to choose from after all! As long as you proceed with your basic values in place, you will not stray far from what you truly want and will eventually arrive at the pinnacle of achieving your goals. As your values and goals change and evolve, simply adjust your plan as necessary to stay in alignment with them, while still nurturing a sense of comfort, security, and fulfillment. You will know that you are moving toward what you want because you know what it is that you want. When you are aware of what you truly value in life, you are empowered to find ways to achieve it. Without this basic connection, you just muddle along and get nowhere.

REFLECTION QUESTIONS

How clearly defined were your own values when you began college? How did that relate to your academic performance?

For Your Journal

VALUES AND LEARNING

*Please respond to the following in your journal or by using the **Journal Module** on the CW.*

Knowing your values is truly invaluable. Attempting to navigate life without clear values can cause depression and feelings of hopelessness. If you find that you do not have a strong value system to guide you, then perhaps this next exercise will help you establish a few simple principles to live and learn by. The exercise asks that you articulate and examine your basic values as they relate to the topic of *learning.* First, answer the questions. Then develop a statement that clearly describes the values you hold about learning.

1. Who or what has influenced or informed your thoughts and feelings about getting a college education? Please list the names or situations.

2. List three reasons why you decided to come to college. (For example, phrase your response as "I am attending college because I value _____ " and fill in the blank with your reason.

3. Describe the source of your motivation for doing your very best in college.

4. Do you think it is important to be a good learner? Why or why not?

5. What are your priorities when it comes to devoting time and energy to your studies?

Using your answers, develop a **values statement** about learning. You can begin your statement like this: *"I value these three things about my college education . . ."*

Then try this opener: *"Learning is important because . . ."*

Remember, your personal values should ring true in your own heart and mind. You may find that your valuation of learning and education is not directly associated with any personal values you are aware of. If you are just accepting someone else's values, you will not have much energy to support your statements. When you "own" your values, they will be easily recognized by a feeling of clarity and certainty.

Student Perspective

SELF-ESTEEM

I recall the very important moment in my life when I began to understand the value of self-worth. I lived most of my young life under the assumption that I was OK with myself and was a generally content individual. One evening, I was absolutely staggered when a fellow student, during a philosophical discussion, accused me of "verging on martyrdom" and claimed that I was not really happy. Of course, I was stunned. What would make him say such a thing? He then said that in all of the time he had known me, he had never seen me turn down an extra credit assignment or decline to do someone a favor. I argued that this was no reason to assume I was unhappy—I was just a hard worker and liked to help others. What was wrong with that? Then, he asked me if I actually enjoyed doing the extra work, or if I just craved the attention and praise. At this, I balked and didn't respond. Instead, I urged him to offer more examples to support his original accusation.

He proceeded to ask me where I had gotten the lovely shirt I was wearing. This seemingly ridiculous question intended to "get him off the hook" only angered me further. Looking down at my shirt, I replied that he was an idiot. I had owned this ratty old shirt for many years—there was nothing lovely about it. He smiled and told me that I had just proven his claim—I could not accept a compliment either. My problem, he said, was that I did not value myself. Not only was I unhappy, but I also was unable to see the unhappiness because my sense of self-worth was not strong enough. I left the meeting thinking what an absolute jerk he was, and I tried to get the entire ludicrous conversation out of my mind.

Later in the evening, I found myself pondering the debate and wondering why he might think such things. What exactly was it that he saw in me that I could not see? After several hours, I began to understand. How often did I tell someone that I was "fine" when I really wasn't because I thought my feelings would not matter or be cared about? How frequently did I refuse, ignore, or downplay compliments offered to me? How envious was I when I'd hear about a party I could not attend? How often had I called myself "stupid," made jokes about my shortcomings, or complained about my workload? How many times had I helped a friend before taking care of work I had to do for myself?

When I really sat down and took a long, honest look at myself, all of these questions were easily answered—I did all of these things too often. I realized that I felt uncomfortable when someone said "Good job" or "You look very nice today" because I could not see it. I had to face the fact that I was constantly feeling overburdened by my responsibilities, but instead of admitting it and lightening my load, I pressed harder and added more work—as if I had something to prove. I downplayed my intelligence and skills when talking to others because I was afraid of them thinking that I was arrogant. There were a million different ways, every single day, that I was sabotaging myself, my efforts, and my happiness. I was working in a job I hated just for the money. I was helping friends and family every day with different things, yet struggling to rush and finish my homework at 3 A.M. That jerk was right—I did not value myself enough to see these things. I was so concerned about how others saw me, what they thought, how I could make them feel, and what I could do to impress them that I did not even think about my own needs or feelings. I had become unimportant to myself—and I was unhappy.

That night, I began the difficult process of reassessing my motivation and personal values. This is very hard to do, and I am still, years later, working on it. When I make a decision, I have to stop and ask myself how the choice I am making will make *me* feel, what benefits it will bring to *me*, and whether or not it is what I really want for *myself*. When my best friend asks me to do her a favor, I first consider my own time limitations, plans, and needs before agreeing to do something that might interfere with my activities. Instead of just staying at my miserable job, I thought about what type of work makes me happy and how important my salary is—then, I made the choice to change jobs. I examined my college activities and decided to keep the ones I really enjoy and eliminate the others. My approach to life has changed considerably since that night at the meeting. Now, I can honestly say that I am happy with my life, and I am in touch with my own sense of self-worth.

Initially, I felt very selfish. But over time, I realized that the only things I do to the best of my ability and with joy and fulfillment are those things that I feel personally motivated to do. I only have so many hours in a day to devote to the various responsibilities and tasks I set for myself. With an increased sense of my own worth and value, I now understand that this time is precious and should be spent as carefully and rewardingly as possible.

REFLECTION QUESTIONS

1. Comment on an example from your life that shows how your self-worth or self-esteem influences your reactions to praise or criticism.

2. What is the difference between someone being selfish and someone having high self-esteem?

SUMMARY

This chapter introduced the concept of **self-directed learning** and the idea that your ability to learn is shaped by your *feelings about and value* of the learning process. Self-directed learning presumes that you are learning because you want to and that you take full responsibility for deepening your own learning process. Self-directed learning asks you to understand why you learn before you can create learning experiences and requires you to develop and practice a highly open state. It also requires that you articulate and understand your personal values.

Values are powerful invisible influences that affect the way we think, feel, and act. They determine what is meaningful to us. They are instilled in us from an early age, but they can also be highly situational and redefined with time and experience.

Core values are basic and universal. They typically transcend culture, upbringing, media, and peers. The ultimate core value that the majority of the human race instinctively shares is the value of life.

Situational values can change. Your actions and values are not always in alignment. You may occasionally find yourself in a conflicting situation, where you are espousing certain values, but due to the situation, you are acting in a manner that does not represent your values. Personal values should ring true in your own heart and mind. These values inform your opinions, and your opinions shape your decisions. When you are clear about and aware of your values, you are better prepared to make **conscious choices.**

The first and probably the only necessary step in planning is to know what you want to accomplish in each area of your life. Stating your **goals** as something you will do and making a plan to do it in a specific amount of time not only helps you to remember what's important, but it is also the beginning of becoming accountable. Although being in alignment with your personal values and goals may not be possible all of the time, a *simple moment of reflection* prior to making a decision can create the possibility of alignment.

Case Studies

CASE STUDY 1.1

Rally Financial Group:
Organizational Values and Principles

Organizational principles and values are essential components of the business structure of most companies. In this case study, you are asked to prepare for a job interview by comparing your personal values and goals with the values and principles outlined for the Rally Financial Group.

Consider yourself a prospective employee of the Rally Financial Group. Prior to your interview, you researched the company's mission statement on-line. Discuss why you would or would not choose to work for this company based strictly on the compatibility of your personal values and goals with those of the company. Which, if any, of your values might become *situational* if you did take a job with this firm?

RALLY FINANCIAL GROUP

Statement of Organizational Values and Principles

Our executives are expected to be role models and set appropriate examples in accordance with our organizational values and principles. They guide how we do our jobs and focus our common work ethics. They are our defining edge and set us apart from our competitors. All employees should practice these values and principles in their daily tasks and their interactions with customers and staff.

VALUE	PRINCIPLE
Integrity. We act in accordance with our words and values. We respect the laws and good business practices of the countries in which we operate.	We abstain from any practice that is illegal and violates fair trade.
Diversity. We accommodate personal and professional differences.	Lifestyle, religious, and cultural differences are tolerated with respect and acceptance.
Collaboration. Teamwork is paramount to each employee's success.	Participation is an integral part of the decision-making process.
Profits. We value profits over personal relationships.	Cost effectiveness and working within established budget parameters are continuing priorities over customer service.

CASE STUDY 1.2

College Values and Principles

Part One.   Colleges are also businesses. Most have selected core values or principles that support their mission as an educational institution. For this case study, locate your college's mission statement and any related values and principles. Try locating this information on the college Internet site or in the college catalog. Another possible way to locate your college's values and principles is to interview a college administrator such as the provost, a dean, or a vice president.

Part Two.   Review your college's values and principles. Consider your personal values in relation to the college's position. Select one of the college's values or principles to add to your own value system. Be specific and provide an example of how or what you have to change to come fully in alignment with this new value.

Discuss how realistic the college values and principles are. Can you cite evidence that the institution, instructors, and staff are acting in alignment with these values and principles? What do you think would have to change to make the college as a whole adopt the principles they espouse? Discuss your answers with the class or your discussion group.

Demonstration of Competency

*Please respond to the following in your journal or by using the **Demonstration of Competency Module** on the CW.*

This chapter has asked you to articulate your personal values and state your goals. To evaluate your mastery of the concepts and your commitment to apply your values and goals to day-to-day situations, your demonstration of competency is to *set a learning goal that exceeds your current ability.* Make sure that the learning goal is realistic and can be achieved in less than one week. This learning goal should require you to abide by your values and do something you have not done previously in relation to your learning. For example, a learning goal might be to have a conference with the instructor of a class that is difficult. Another example of exceeding your current abilities might be to reread a tough assignment and then explain it to someone. It could also be something like completing your homework before your e-mail.

Your written essay on this experience will serve as your demonstration of competency.

Additional references and resources for chapter topics can be found at **www.prenhall.com/gray**.

Choices

CRITICAL THINKING

Sometimes, we hit a fork in the road and realize that a choice must be made. And then sometimes, we mistake it for a spoon and miss our turn without ever knowing it.

—SHARON AINSLEY, STUDENT PERSPECTIVES AUTHOR

How did you get here and what will you do now? From the moment you were born, choices have been made for you, with you, and by you. The most profound outcome of all of these choices is that the sum total of your choices has brought you right here, right now. When you think about it, you have traveled a very long and winding path to be here! The questions are: How actively did you participate in the process of bringing yourself to this point in your life? How much involvement do you want in creating your future?

This chapter focuses on how various influences impact your decision-making process and directly affect the course of your life. When you allow others to make your choices for you, you can be setting yourself up for narrowly defined outcomes that may not serve your best interest. Critical thinking enables you to make informed choices that are balanced with inner guidance. The first step to approaching self-responsible decision making is to become aware of how often you are given the opportunity to choose.

What If . . .

What if you finish reading this chapter before you do anything else? Do you think that is a possibility you can actualize?

Try This

IMAGINING CHOICES

Imagine what might happen if you decide to choose to do something different right now. Write down two activities you could be doing right now instead of reading this. Continue writing about what possibly could happen in the next three hours for each of the two activities. Then, stretch your imagination and write about how the consequences of the two activities could impact the next three days. Really try to follow the thread of several possible effects of your choices over time. Then, if you want to be really imaginative, see if you can think of how these choices today might affect the next three years.

One thing is certain, you cannot even begin to conceive of all the possible outcomes from all of the choices you make in a single day, much less a week, a year, a life. What you can do is *practice noticing that you are choosing* the direction of your life in the moment-to-moment actions and thoughts you make every day.

THE MOMENT OF CHOICE

The moment of choice is always now. The key to the moment of choice is that you must first recognize that you have a choice in every moment. Situations may arise where you feel trapped or controlled by some external force or fate. You may not be able to change a situation, but *you can choose how to respond to it*. What does this mean? This is where the concept of "response-ability" comes from. Responding with awareness is very different than reacting from habit. *The moment of choice is an instance where you realize you have several options and consciously decide to participate in the outcome of an internal or external situation.*

An example of an internal situation is how your thoughts and emotions interpret an event. The external situations are your actions, interactions, or behaviors with the situation. For example, some people may feel trapped in dead-end jobs. They have to keep working to pay bills. If they take any extra time off from work to look for new jobs, their pay might be reduced or they might be fired. The internal situation is how frustrated these people feel. The external situation occurs when they speak with coworkers about their frustration and complain about management. They also have an internal situation when they think about the job. Their thoughts may focus on complaining to a district manager. Each day, those in the dead-end jobs do not believe that they have any choice but to keep going to work. They choose over and over again to suffer and complain about the situation. Every time coworkers see them coming, they know they will hear complaints about how tough the boss is and how frustrating life is. If you asked these people why they don't simply quit and get another job, their reply might be that they have no choice but to stay there and work because they have to pay bills. The point here is that they do not feel that they have any choice but to keep doing the same thing.

Most moments of choice are missed simply because you do not notice that those moments are potential turning points where you could change or reaffirm the direction of your life. If the people with the dead-end jobs decided to call in sick one day so they could go look for new jobs, everything *could* change. If they decided to stop complaining to coworkers and instead started networking by asking about leads for possible employment, everything could change. Their external situation is then directly affected by their internal choice.

For Your Journal

MOMENT OF CHOICE

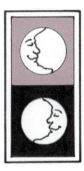

*Please respond to the following in your journal or by using the **Journal Module** on the CW.*

Consider this statement and reflect on its meaning: A moment of choice is not a choice unless you are aware of it. See if you can identify a situation in your life where you feel you have "no choice." For example, you may feel you have no choice about your current living conditions because of your limited finances. Reexamine the situation and see if you can come up with several possible choices you may have overlooked.

CHOICE IS OPPORTUNITY

Many turning points or possible choices sneak up on us and we miss the opportunity to choose. We tend to see choices only when they are obvious, like choosing what to order from a menu at a restaurant. We know we must make choices about how we spend money, who we associate with, how we use our time, what we eat, and how we dress, but we can miss the more subtle moments of choice that arise, like what tone of voice we use, or the thoughts we have about ourselves or others. Instead of consciously participating in decisions, choices are made for us by default or by the momentum of our unconscious, habituated agendas that push us along in the same rut or pattern. For example, a student always avoids situations where she might be called on to speak in front of a group. In class, she sits in the back of the room and avoids making eye contact with the instructor because she doesn't want him to think she is interested in participating. That unconscious choice has long-term effects that she is unaware of. It limits the type of learning experiences she has and limits the quality of the interaction she has with her classmates. Although she should use the classroom situation to practice speaking in front of her peers, the habitual fear of speaking wins out.

When an event occurs, we tend to have a natural, automatic response that surfaces as our initial reaction. When it rains, it can spoil our mood; when we are insulted, we retaliate. Without *conscious* intervention, the reaction simply "happens"—whether it is appropriate or not. We are tied to a repetitive structure of automatic action and reaction. We usually do only what we think we should be doing or what we are conditioned to do without giving it much thought. For example, making additional time to study for a midterm may be hampered by a conditioned response of watching TV until 10 P.M. It does not occur to us that we could do things differently by simply making different choices. Consider the saying, "If you want to keep getting what you are getting, keep doing what you are doing."

To begin to see choice as an opportunity, we must actively move against the repetitive current of automatic reactions and thoughts. Creating self-change is an art and a skill. Anyone who has tried to stop smoking knows that for a lasting change to be made, he must choose against the grain of his automatic responses many, many times. Maintaining a choice that creates change means renewing efforts in the face of failures or setbacks. Every opportunity to choose is a chance to change, as illustrated in Figure 2.1.

CHOICE MAKES US RESPONSIBLE

The sense of personal responsibility connected to making choices can be either overwhelming or empowering. It is certainly overwhelming when you are not clear about your intentions, values, or goals. This makes moment-to-moment choices very confusing—you are more likely to let circumstances decide for you. This approach serves to let you off the hook and avoid the efforts needed to make clear-minded, tough decisions—and the possibility that you might have to face being *wrong*.

Choice and the process of self-change.   FIGURE 2.1

```
┌─────────────────────┐        ┌────────┐        ┌─────────────────────┐
│     AWARENESS       │───────▶│ choice │───────▶│       PLAN          │
│ Knowing why to change│        └────────┘        │   How to change     │
└─────────────────────┘            │             └─────────────────────┘
        ▲                          ▼                        │
        │                   ┌──────────────┐                ▼
   ┌────────┐               │  RESULTS OF  │           ┌────────┐
   │ choice │──────────────▶│   CHOICES    │◀──────────│ choice │
   └────────┘               └──────────────┘           └────────┘
        ▲                          ▲                        │
        │                          │                        ▼
┌─────────────────────┐        ┌────────┐        ┌─────────────────────┐
│    DETERMINATION     │◀───────│ choice │◀───────│      ACTION         │
│When to repeat the process│    └────────┘        │   What to change    │
└─────────────────────┘                           └─────────────────────┘
```

Each choice in the process adds to the magnitude and stability of the change.

When you begin to realize that making a mistake or a wrong choice can be another method of learning, then you are more likely to risk taking on more responsibility. Clarity about your goals and values acts as

We discover what works by finding out what doesn't work; those who never made a mistake, never made a discovery.

—SAMUEL SMILES

ongoing inner guidance to your decision-making process. You actually feel free or more spontaneous with your ability to choose when you accept responsibility for making choices that support your aims or plans.

You become more confident in your decision-making skills when you use them more often.

INFLUENCED CHOICES

Choices are influenced by many of the same elements that determine values. Many influences are positive resources and provide guidance. Other influences are habituated and based on unsubstantiated opinions that lack firm evidence. To move from the level of *influenced choices* to one of *informed choices,* the first step is to become aware of the power that external situations and people have over our life decisions. If we acknowledge our influences, we can examine them for their appropriateness and become aware of any *unconscious assumptions* that are tied to them. Unconscious or unexamined assumptions can be the source of *unwarranted assertions*—ideas and beliefs that are not grounded in much more than hearsay. For example, visit any new car lot. Judging by the gas mileage, price range, and size of the vehicles, what are some of the assumptions that car manufacturers are making about their potential customers? An example of a resulting unwarranted assertion is that Americans want to drive larger cars with lower gas mileage.

Perhaps not so obvious are the unconscious assumptions that arise when there are contrasting opinions. For example, when discussing a health care issue, one person assumes that Western medicine views all disease treatment as either surgical or pharmaceutical. Based on this assumption, the person argues that traditional doctors do not consider nutrition and diet as important as does a holistic practitioner. Their second assumption is that a holistic practitioner might look at diet as a treatment instead of using herbs or other remedies. Another example of unconscious assumptions is reflected in how we feel about our personal abilities and aptitudes. We may assume that we are not good writers because our papers have red marks and comments on how to improve our grammar. If we act from that assumption, we might choose to avoid other courses that require intensive written work. Unwarranted assertions remain powerful influences on our moment-to-moment decisions when we lose sight of their subjectivity and begin to accept them as factual.

Not all assumptions are erroneous or a bad influence. Assumptions are most risky when they are unconscious. A good question to ask yourself would be *What are my assumptions?* We have to make assumptions to accomplish even simple tasks. For example, we assume that the driver next to us will not unexpectedly change lanes. Most times, this assumption is correct because it is based logically on our day-to-day experiences. When we make assumptions based on reliable and proven authorities, we are making *informed choices.*

Student Perspective

RECOGNIZING ASSUMPTIONS

Relying on preconceptions and assumptions can be one of the most detrimental aspects of your intellectual life. When you were a senior in high school and planning for the future, you probably chose a college based on what friends said, or on what your parents and teachers told you. Maybe you even decided on your major because of what others said about the earnings, job potential, or ease of work. You might choose your courses from one semester to the next based on what friends tell you about the difficulty of certain courses they have taken. Every day, you take in opinions from the people around you and other sources. The questions are: To what should you give credibility? Should you listen? Well, yes . . . and no.

Imagine that your best friend took a political science class last semester and did horribly. She explains to you that the professor is a jerk, the work is hard, and the grading policy is unfair. For your own good, she urges you not to enroll in the course. What do you do? This is the time for some real critical-thinking skills. You cannot base your choice on someone else's understanding of a situation if you are going to create your own experience; you must develop your own understanding. You might start by asking yourself how much credence you can put in what your friend has told you. Maybe she is not such a good student and did poorly because she did not study and do her work. Maybe she and the professor had a misunderstanding at some point that made their relationship a little shaky. The point is, you don't know. Before assuming anything about this class and professor, do your own research. Talk to other students. Set up a meeting with the professor. Ask to see the syllabus. Look over the textbook. Determine for yourself what you feel is true about the situation, then act in accordance with your own understandings.

If you still cannot make a firm choice based on the information available, clear all of it out of your perception and start fresh. A blank slate is better than one that is full of other people's (possibly inaccurate) opinions. The last thing you want to do is miss out on a good class because of what someone else said. Even worse, you could take the class, but *create* a negative experience for yourself because you let your assumptions kill it before you even begin. Chances are if you walk into class believing the professor is a jerk, you will find a jerk—not because he really is one, but because your perception is already decided and you aren't even going to give him a chance. If you remain aware of your assumptions and determine your own understanding before making your choices—you might just find a wonderful experience waiting for you; an experience you would have lost had you just listened to what someone else had to say.

(text continued on p. 34)

For Your Journal

ACCOUNTING FOR INFLUENCES

*Please respond to the following in your journal or by using the **Journal Module** on the CW.*

Part A   Carefully consider each *influencer* and determine whether it might be a high, medium, or low influence on your decision-making process for each situation listed. For the purpose of this exercise, influencers are people, institutions, or events that shape or support your belief system. Also, add any of your own personal influencers that do not appear on the list. Remember, some influencers are unconscious. The objective of this exercise is to recognize and acknowledge *all* influencers—to become aware of the influencers you have not realized are affecting your choices.

SCENARIOS

Scenario A: You are trying to decide whether to accept a full scholarship to pursue your master's degree or take a full-time job working in your field.

Scenario B: You are deciding which over-the-counter medication to buy.

Scenario C: You are deciding on a college major.

Scenario D: You have just been told that your car was stolen and you are deciding how to respond.

Scenario E: You are about to vote in a presidential election and you are deciding who to vote for.

INFLUENCERS	SCENARIOS				
For each Scenario rate the influencers as H (high), M (medium), or L (low)	A	B	C	D	E
Parents or family members					
Friends or peers					
Movies: actors or characters					
TV: programs, commercials					
Print media: books, papers, magazines					
Religion or spiritual practices					
Personal experiences					
Music: lyrics, artists					
Other:					
Other:					

Part B   Uncovering hidden assumptions is the next step in the process of acknowledging your influencers. Let's take this examination to the next level. A low influence might be very subtle, but its presence in your decision-making process has an impact. For each scenario, list one of the influencers you rated as low in the middle column of the chart below. In the right-hand column, note the "how, why, or what" (assumption) of the influencer. Ask yourself the question, "How would this influencer affect my decision?"

Here is an example for further guidance:

SCENARIO	LOW INFLUENCER	ASSUMPTION
C	Movie	Almost all of the movies I have seen involving stolen cars show they end up getting wrecked. My assumption is that if my car is stolen, it will be ruined. I will have to buy another one.

SCENARIO	LOW INFLUENCER	ASSUMPTION
A		
B		
C		
D		
E		

Reviewing your influencers and how they directly or indirectly affect your choices is an ongoing process. As you gain insight into your unexamined assumptions, you might begin to question whether some of your influencers are still appropriate and whether you should consider widening your sphere of influence to include *informed choices.*

REFLECTION QUESTIONS

Think of some examples of times when you have trusted someone else's opinion and allowed yourself to be influenced by what he or she said. Was he or she right about the situation? Did you discover that your assumptions were wrong? What happened?

CRITICAL THINKING AND CHOICES

Critical thinking is the art of choosing what to believe and what not to believe. It has been defined as living the *examined life.* Becoming aware of the source of our opinions is the first step in examining our assumptions. Critical thinkers are willing to look at the validity of their opinions and stay open-minded by considering new information. Informed choices are made based on logical and supported evidence. By questioning, analyzing, and evaluating situations and information before deciding or judging, critical thinkers attempt to distinguish between facts and opinions.

INFORMED CHOICES

Informed choices use components of critical thinking to help the decision-making process. Critical thinking evaluates ideas and tests evidence, checking assertions for credibility and reasonableness.

Following are three guiding principles (illustrated in Figure 2.2) for making an *informed choice.*

1. Examine your influences. This means being willing to ask questions and take nothing for granted. Question your assumptions and the assumptions of others to help you distinguish fact from opinion. Like a good lawyer, critical thinkers look for evidence to support statements that are offered as factual. *Many opinions are disguised as facts.* If it is not clear that a given statement is a fact (e.g., the sun rises in the east), then treat the statement as an opinion (e.g., the sun rarely shines in Seattle). Assumptions can be based on beliefs or opinions that may or may not be well founded. Carefully examine the evidence, facts, or opinions underlying your assumptions and the assumptions of those who influence you.

2. Review and reflect on your personal experience. If you have experiences that relate to the choices you are making, be aware of possible errors in perception. Remember that personal experience is a valuable influ-

The basis of informed choices.   **FIGURE 2.2**

INFORMED CHOICE

Examine Influences

Review Experience

Research Authorities

ence, but you interpret your experiences through the lens of your emotions, physical sensations, and thoughts. For example, one person's experience of riding a roller coaster is felt as exhilaration, while another person's perceptual lens of this experience is fear and sickness. Using this same example, you can also see how even an accurate experiential perception can become outdated. Your first experience on a roller coaster as a child may have been one mixed with fear and excitement. As an adult, you experience fearlessness and wild abandon.

Your perceptions are relative to your belief systems as well. What one person perceives as innocent, another person views as unethical. Copying movies to a DVD is considered fair game by some and illegal by others. Consider the lens of your perception as a potential limiting factor, and be willing to be open-minded. Is it possible that even opposing opinions could both be valid? Look at your experiences and the reported experiences of others from several points of view. *Try to step outside your personal interpretations and look at the experience from multiple perspectives.*

3. Research the reliability of authorities. How do you qualify a reliable authority? The media uses authorities to influence consumers and build interesting news stories. What makes an authority trustworthy? Statistics and status are the typical qualifiers for determining the validity of an authority. Authorities can be people like doctors, lawyers, sports figures, film and TV celebrities, and other experts. Authorities often contradict each other or are paid for their comments, endorsing products for a fee. When thinking critically about the authority's credibility, focus on the quality of the evidence they offer to support their opinions or expertise. Two rules for researching the reliability of authorities are:

1. How recent or historical is the supporting evidence? A viable opinion from an authority generally references both historical and recent examples or research. In other words, the range of support for the opinion is grounded and proven *over time.*
2. Are there additional independent statistics, growing bodies of evidence, or personal testimonies to support the authority?

CHOICES AND DEMOCRACY

When you think about the effort required to test evidence and opinions, it is easy to understand how you might prefer to blindly accept the assumptions, assertions, or opinions of others. In many cases, you may base your opinions on how you *feel* about the topic. It is easier than doing all of the work necessary to develop an informed opinion. Yet, if you do not make the effort to be informed, you sacrifice your freedom to choose. One of the most frequently cited reasons for not voting is the amount of effort required to research the candidates. Thinking about doing this much research before casting a ballot can discourage people from the voting process. It is hard to know what or who to believe, where to find true answers, or which sources of information are accurate. Some people become so frustrated and overwhelmed that they do not participate in the democratic process. Yet by not participating, they relinquish their power to affect their circumstances, improve society, and bring about change in their communities. Unfortunately, the price paid for such indifference can be quite high. Researching the credibility and reliability of authorities is an ongoing personal responsibility—a necessary part of making an informed choice and maintaining a democracy.

FOLLOWING YOUR HEART

What Is Intuition?

In contrast to critical-thinking skills, intuition is knowing without thinking. Everyone uses intuition to some degree when making choices. The better you understand how your intuition works, the more attuned you are to noticing how your body signals you through the intuitive process. The intuitive process is determined by how you *feel* about a decision or choice. For example, if you get lost in a housing subdivision while trying to find your way to a friend's home and you do not have a map or cell phone, intuition might give you a sense of which way to turn. Another example of intuition is your "gut feelings" about a person's character. Many people are not trained to be sensitive to intuition; instead, they tend to second-guess or deny it. Intuition becomes a less reliable source when you are filled with self-doubt.

Intuition is the really important thing.

—ALBERT EINSTEIN

Here are three guidelines to help you recognize how your intuition can guide your decision-making process.

- Intuition is described as a clear knowing, an insight or knowledge gained without information. It is also referred to as inner guidance. To be receptive to this way of knowing, you must have some method of quieting your mind. Cultivate a state of "no thought" when you wish to empower your intuitive side.
- Observe how you feel as you make decisions. Do you feel calm or anxious? Paralyzed or confident? Drained or energized? If the way you feel about a decision does not seem relaxed or energizing, your intuition may be trying to guide you in another direction.
- Ignore inner voices that say "You should . . . ." This is not intuition speaking. Intuition is not based on fear or guilt. It is a wordless sense of something being correct or incorrect.

If you want a hot cup of tea, first you must empty your cup.

—CHINESE PROVERB

Ambiguity and Clarity

Informed choices and intuition are not all you need to make good decisions—you must also acknowledge the importance of being comfortable with *ambiguity*. Ambiguity is uncertainty—a state of not knowing. Admitting that you are unsure or that you don't know is different from being confused. Being confused is like trying to sit between two chairs—it can have a very uncomfortable, frustrating feeling. Being comfortable with ambiguity or not knowing makes it possible to see things from new perspectives, ask potent questions, and quiet your thinking to receive intuitive guidance.

Clarity is a state that can come in fleeting glimpses. Clarity is best described as seeing the big picture or understanding the interrelationships of many perspectives at once. Ideally, we would make all of our decisions from a state of clarity. However, clarity also implies we know something to be true. For purposes of this book, we will confine our search for truth to ourselves. Clarity means knowing we are making choices that are in alignment with our values and goals.

It is the mark of an educated mind to be able to entertain a thought without accepting it.

—ARISTOTLE

Student Perspective

SELF-CONFIDENCE AND THE WILLINGNESS TO ASK QUESTIONS

You have most likely experienced the phenomenon of sitting in class and hearing the professor ask, "Does everyone understand this?" When is the last time you raised your hand and said, "No, could you please go over that one more time?" When is the last time you really didn't understand and should have raised your hand, but simply let the class proceed without speaking up and asking for help? When is the last time someone said, "Are you sure?" and you said "Yes" when you really weren't? This is a common occurrence, and is, to some degree, a reflection of a lack of self-confidence you may be feeling at the moment. Here you are in college, expected to know what is going on—why would you go and make yourself look stupid by admitting you don't understand something? Well for starters, self-confident, self-responsible students will admit they don't "get it" simply because their goal is to "get it." They know that they don't have a chance of improving their understanding unless they admit that they don't understand.

It is really helpful to talk to those who can help you because then you have support and assistance in your efforts and are far more likely to figure it out. But if you don't speak up and say, "I don't know" or "I'm not sure," you will never get help and may never gain the understanding you seek. If you go on pretending to understand something, eventually you will be expected to demonstrate your knowledge—and you wont' be able to. Failing or falling short of the mark will just decrease your confidence level even more. Why put yourself through all that? The minute you accept the fact that you don't really understand or are not sure about something (and that is OK), you open the door to making progress. Stay confident in your ability to learn—just because something doesn't "click" right away does not mean you cannot figure it out. Having to ask questions, consider several possibilities, or seek help does not mean you are stupid; rather, it means you are making a real effort—and that is the sign of a truly self-empowered student.

REFLECTION QUESTIONS

Can you think of a time when you should have admitted you didn't understand something, but you kept quiet and eventually paid the price? What was the price? How did you resolve your situation?

INTEGRATED CHOICES

Combining critical thinking with intuition creates integrated choices. This is often referred to as balancing the head with the heart. Calling on both of these aspects of yourself in decision-making situations widens the scope of your resources. This approach considers not only such things as facts and research, but also people and feelings. Integrated choices are also conscious choices; they are made with self-awareness and self-responsibility. Integrated choices come with understanding that choices have both short-term and long-term consequences. You choose consciously when you examine your assumptions and influences to see the possible effects of your actions and thoughts on others and yourself.

Try This

ACCOUNTING FOR INTEGRATED CHOICES

Can you cite an example of how you have used a combination of critical thinking and intuition when making a recent decision? For example, perhaps you have decided to take a trip over spring break. You have researched the opinions of friends about possible safe, fun, and reasonably priced locations. You also have used your personal experiences of past spring break trips to narrow the list of potential destinations. When deciding between two places, you use your intuition to select the place you will visit. Describe where you used critical-thinking skills and inner knowing, or intuition, to make a choice.

RESPONSE-ABILITY

An integrated choice works from the premise that you can, to a large degree, choose your thoughts and feelings—that you are "response-able." It is important to understand that opportunities to make integrated choices are not limited to the "easy things." Using self-awareness empowers you to choose your thoughts or feelings so that they are in alignment with your goals, values, and principles. This is accomplished by first being aware of what you are thinking and feeling, and then deciding if these thoughts and emotions are appropriate to the circumstances at hand. When you have accomplished this level of awareness and control, you are then "response-able."

You don't get to choose how or when you are going to die. You only get to choose how you are going to live.

—JOAN BAEZ

Student Perspective

ASSUMPTIONS AND THE POWER TO CHOOSE

It was not until I approached the college environment that I truly understood how powerful choice was in life. While experiencing my own unique life circumstances and dealing with my own set of difficult obstacles, I had never given much direct thought to the idea of choice—I just accepted that some things were out of my control. Life seems, most times, to simply "flow" without much regard for our intentions, needs, or desires. Often, it is not at all obvious that the choices we make impact our lives so deeply. Sometimes, it isn't even obvious that we have certain choices available to us at all.

We can easily acknowledge that we have many small choices to make throughout the day. We choose what to eat in the morning, which route to drive to school, or which outfit to wear. We might also identify with larger choices such as whether or not we will get married, have children, change schools, or relocate. The thing I discovered about my own understanding of "choice" as a concept was that everything I connected to the idea was an action or activity: eating, sleeping, driving, dating. All of the things that I understood as choices were physical, tangible activities that were easily controlled. What I did not see was that the realm of choice—and the true power it holds—lies in the deeper, intangible areas of thought, emotion, and self-awareness.

Like many of my peers, I entered college with a set of preconceptions about my abilities, my aptitudes, my interests, and myself that were forged by and rooted in my past experiences. Every obstacle I ever faced, every problem I ever encountered, and every misfortune that ever befell me were things that I considered to be simply a part of "my lot in life." My self-awareness was tainted with feelings of fear, inadequacy, self-pity, and injustice—all due to things that I viewed as circumstances beyond my control. But I was wrong.

As I began to truly examine my choices, I came upon a startling revelation: choice was not confined to simple activities and actions. In a single moment, there might be a hundred different courses of action to choose from, but submerged just beneath those actions are a hundred different thoughts, ideas, and feelings that drive us to act. I realized that I allowed these underlying choices to be subconsciously decided—I was only really involved with the action part. I was relinquishing control in a sense because I was not actively participating in the motivational, meaningful aspect of the choices at hand. I was choosing what to wear but never asking myself, "Why?" I was choosing what to do on Friday night, but not choosing to connect my purpose, intent, or values to the action. Worst of all, I was choosing to allow my past to make choices for me in the present because I was not acknowledging my power to intervene in my own thought process.

In just that single day, with that newfound understanding of choice, everything changed. I stopped accepting the position of "victim of circumstance" and accepted responsibility for choosing to choose. I now realize that I am the one with the power to choose how I view myself as a person, what my talents are, and what my future holds. I determine what my next move is based on consciously chosen thoughts—not autonomous, habitual ones. There is a distinction between events that are out of my control and my reactions to those events, which are very much my choice. Whatever the circumstance, it is within my power to make choices to think, feel, and concentrate my attention on positive, productive things rather than dwell in misfortune or negativity. I realize that if I am feeling sad, I am not condemned to keep feeling sad—I can choose to refocus and improve my mood. Many emotions such as anger, fear, regret, and anxiety can be faced the same way—I can choose to redirect myself and change my reaction. Thoughts and ideas are chosen and directed to align with my goals and aspirations. I am not powerless anymore. I have found the simplest, and the greatest, self-empowerment tool I have ever encountered—the power to choose.

REFLECTION QUESTIONS

Discuss a time when you made a life-changing choice. Can you remember the criteria you used to decide? What skills might you use to make future decisions differently?

SUMMARY

This chapter explored the inner and outer worlds of **choices** and the **critical-thinking skills** necessary to make those choices. It is through your personal series of choices that your life has progressed to this point. The choices you make will directly affect your future. Critical thinking requires that you examine your influences, uncover your assumptions, and review your experiences before making a decision. Critical thinking is the means by which you make **informed choices.**

Even in seemingly "powerless" situations, you can make choices of your thoughts, feelings, and reactions that will help you gain control. Simply knowing that choices exist is a first step; you must then learn how to make the best, most informed choices for your values and goals. This requires that you learn to be actively engaged in these choices and to recognize your **influences** and **assumptions** while determining the right choice for you.

In your life, there are many influences or outside entities that contribute to your ideas. **Influenced choices** are those motivated from outside yourself, including:

- family
- friends
- media
- culture
- religion

The influences play a huge role in determining what you think, believe, and—essentially—who you are. It is not unusual to find that one or more of your influences have been hindering you, making choices for you, or even forcing you to make poor choices. You may discover that certain influences have embedded **assumptions,** or preconceived ideas not based in truth, that affect the way you make your choices. You may also act in response to unwarranted **assertions.** It is important to determine whether an influence or source of information is appropriate, warranted, and valid for you. As you learn to combine and balance your ability to be informed with your ability to trust your inner intuition, you become capable of making **integrated choices** that are personally motivated.

You must be prepared to accept **responsibility** for your choices, good or bad. Remember, mistakes are merely opportunities for learning. It might seem easier or safer in some situations to avoid making a choice or to respond out of habit, but you must remember that in doing so, you are giving up your right to control the outcome of the situation. If your intention is to achieve a goal or attain some level of success, you cannot afford to relinquish the great power you possess—you must remain diligent and alert to the **moments of choice** in your life.

Case Studies

CASE STUDY 2.1

Moment of Decision and Identifying Consequences

Betty is a secretary at a local law firm. Every day, her duties include answering the phones, preparing the schedules for the firm associates, greeting clients, filing paperwork, and other various tasks. She is happy with her job, loves the firm, and enjoys a good salary and benefits.

On Tuesday afternoon, Betty is asked by one of the lawyers to run some errands for him. She is instructed to deliver several files to the courthouse, pick up a set of case histories from a competing firm's office, and then have a set of copies of some new advertising literature made at the local print shop. She sets out at 2 P.M. to start her errands, but must be back to the office for a major administrative meeting by 4 P.M.

As she leaves the parking garage, she notices a street vendor selling perfume and cologne. She ponders for a moment if she should pick up a bottle of that new fragrance she has been wanting for so long. Stopping will consume some of the time she needs to complete her errands. [**first moment of decision**]

She successfully delivers the paperwork to the courthouse and starts off for the office where she must retrieve the stack of case histories. In the reception room, she runs into a woman she went to college with named Joan, who wants to talk with Betty about a possible position as an executive assistant with Joan's firm. Betty ponders the idea of inviting Joan over for dinner, but recalls that Joan had dated Betty's husband a long while back. Suddenly, she finds herself confused about what to do next and somewhat flustered over running into Joan at all. Although inviting her over would be a great opportunity to network with people from this competing law firm, the situation might be emotionally difficult with regard to Betty's husband and may anger her employers and make it look as if she were collaborating with the opposition. [**second moment of decision**]

Realizing that it is now almost 3:30 P.M. and she has yet to make the flyer copies, she heads out to the copy shop. She is trying to hurry, realizing that she is running late and remembering that she must be back to the office in less than half an hour. She approaches the intersection near the copy shop and sees that there is no traffic in either direction, but the light is yellow. By the time she reaches it, it will be red, and this is one of the longest lights in town. Running the light might save her 10 minutes or more and keep her on time, but it is dangerous. [third moment of decision]

Betty returns to the office at 4:25, almost half an hour late for the administrative meeting. Everyone is already in the conference room with the door shut. It is office policy never to interrupt conference room meetings, but she is expected to be part of the discussion and has to go in because she has the case histories they have to review. She stands outside the door for a moment to try to hear what is being discussed and prepare what she will say to her employers. Just then, the door opens up and the senior partner comes out. She must now sufficiently explain her tardiness, but does not wish to disclose the details of her day for fear he may get upset. [fourth moment of decision]

REFLECTION QUESTIONS

1. For each moment of decision, think of at least two possible choices that Betty could make. Describe the possible assumptions that might lead her to each choice and the probable outcome of each choice.

2. For each choice, decide whether it is in alignment with Betty's objectives and goals or if it is a "wrong turn" on her choice path. Explain.

3. If you were Betty, what choices would you make at each moment of decision and why? Try to include an explanation of the reasons and values that relate to each response you give.

4. Discuss the linear progression of the story as it unfolds for Betty. Will the story progress in the same way regardless of the choice made at each moment of decision? Why or why not?

CASE STUDY 2.2
Diversity of Choice and Personal Values

Choice plays a large part in everyone's life. Each day provides unlimited moments in which we are given the opportunity to choose. Attending college is an area of life where choices are very prominent and can mean the difference between success and failure. This will be demonstrated using two very different students, Timothy and Julia.

Timothy made a great effort to prepare for college while in high school, including:

- Choosing courses that would get him ready for the college-level material and taking advance placement courses
- Working toward getting good grades
- Applying for scholarships and starting a savings account to finance his college education
- Completing the forms and paperwork to gain admission to college
- Preparing a plan for his major and learning about which courses were necessary to achieve his goals

For Julia, the notion of going to college came later in life, long after completing high school:

- Because she didn't prepare for college during high school, she was less prepared for the college-level workload and subject material.
- Because she has been working, she does not meet the criteria for most financial assistance such as grants and scholarships and must pay for her classes.
- She did plan and prepare for her major course of study.

DISCUSSION INSTRUCTIONS

Part One

1. Both students are now attending college and pursuing their goals. Different choices on their paths brought them, as individuals, to the same goals. Write a brief list of specific choices that you have made during your journey to begin college.

2. For both Timothy and Julia, there are hundreds of variables, such that if a different choice were made, the outcome might be completely different. If, for example, Timothy never prepared the necessary forms, could he have progressed to the final step? Describe, in your own words, what decisions you made about beginning college that could have turned out differently had you selected another option. Were the decisions you made the best ones for the situations? How did they relate to your values and goals?

3. Every choice you make influences what your next set of options will be. Can you think of any choices from your own experiences of preparing for college that were directly related to other choices you made earlier? Please explain.

Recall that the last steps in the paths for the two students were the same—Timothy and Julia both reached college. Now, let's see what their present set of choices looks like.

Timothy makes only a minimal effort and does not work very hard in his studies, choosing to:

- Select easy courses that do not help him in his major
- Skip classes and do other, more fun, things
- Let his attention drift off during class
- Attend parties and hang out with friends instead of studying
- Fail to complete his homework assignments because they take too much time
- Quit college because he feels like he is a failure

Julia works very hard to be successful in school, choosing to:

- Select courses necessary for her major
- Attend classes, even when it means missing out on something that might be more fun
- Learn ways to focus her attention and get more understanding out of what she is learning
- Learn and practice effective study techniques because she wants to be prepared for exams and quizzes
- Complete all of her homework on time and get help when she needs it
- Get good grades and earn her degree

DISCUSSION INSTRUCTIONS

Part Two

Although Julia and Timothy started at the same place and had the same choices to make, each chose quite differently, with quite different outcomes.

1. For each student, provide one possible direct effect of each of the choices he or she made along the way, and explain whether this effect was what they were trying to achieve. Why or why not?

2. Describe an instance when you were facing similar choices and explain how you chose. What was the result of the choice you made? Was it the best choice for your goals and values?

Demonstration of Competency

SELF-ASSESSMENT

*Please respond to the following in your journal or by using the **Demonstration of Competency Module** on the CW.*

Rate your competency for the concepts listed below using this scale:

> *1 = no experiences or ideas   2 = a few ideas but no experience   3 = some experience*
> *4 = I know all I need to know about this   5 = I am an expert*

Companion
Website

CONCEPT	RATING
Recognizing your influences	
Ability to make informed choices	
Examining assumptions	
Using intuition	
Ability to make conscious decisions	
Comfort with ambiguity	

Set a personal learning objective for any concept that you rated as 1 or 2. Write a sentence stating what you will commit to do and how you plan to learn more about the concept during the next week.

_____

_____

_____

Define these concepts in terms of your own experience.

MOMENT OF CHOICE

_____

_____

INTEGRATED CHOICE OR CONSCIOUS DECISIONS

_____

_____

ASSUMPTIONS

_____

_____

INFORMED CHOICES

_____

_____

INFLUENCED CHOICES

_____

_____

INTUITION

_____

_____

AMBIGUITY

_____

_____

CLARITY

_____

_____

Additional references and resources for chapter topics can be found at **www.prenhall.com/gray**

3

Attention

COMPREHENSION AND FOCUS

To acquire knowledge, one must study; but to acquire wisdom, one must observe.

—MARILYN VOS SAVANT

I n this chapter, you will explore the concept of attention and its relationship to learning. You will increase your awareness of how internal and external distractions detract from your ability to pay attention. With practice, you will find that you can sustain your attention for longer periods and focus it at will. When you strengthen your attention, you improve your observation and comprehension skills.

What If . . .

What if concentration meant a relaxed state of mind and body? What type of efforts do you make when you concentrate on something?

EXPERIENCING ATTENTION

Attention is a quality of focusing, observing, noticing, or concentrating. The idea of attention is very different from the experience of it. This chapter begins with *experiencing* attention and then defines it conceptually.

"Am I here?" Asking yourself this question may seem ridiculous—of course you are here, but are you aware of your surroundings or thoughts? We all have experienced the sensation of being in one place physically while we are mentally or emotionally very far removed. Have you ever been reading a book and then suddenly realized that you cannot remember what the last 10 pages were about? Your eyes were scanning the text, but your attention was elsewhere. Without the ability to fully concentrate, the time necessary to comprehend and remember what you are reading is doubled or tripled, because you end up rereading to retain the information you missed on the first or second pass.

Many times, you are only vaguely aware of what is occurring in your immediate environment because your attention is so inwardly focused on your thoughts and inner conversations. You can drive down a street and visually take in only the street signs or signals necessary to navigate safely, then suddenly realize you have somehow driven miles without really seeing what was out there. Another example is when you are "half listening" to someone. You only vaguely understand enough to nod and say uh-huh. By the end of the conversation, you cannot recount much of what was said. This state of diffused attention borders on a hypnotic trance where you are almost running on automatic pilot. Although it may be appropriate to let your attention run on autopilot while waiting in the checkout line, if you wish to quicken and deepen your learning experiences, sharpening your attention span is necessary.

Try This

ATTENTION ACCOUNTING

Before you begin reading the rest of the chapter, set out a blank sheet of paper and keep a pen handy. Make a firm commitment to yourself and give your very best effort to stay focused on what you are reading here. Carefully and consistently be aware of when your attention wanders to something other than the words on the remaining pages. Every minute or so, ask yourself, "Am I here?" When you notice that your have drifted elsewhere, even for a few seconds, make a note on the paper, then return to your reading. If you have to get up or move away from the area where you are reading, make a note on the paper to describe what caused you to move. If you find your mind wanders, or you are thinking the same thoughts over and over, make a quick note of exactly what type of thought is distracting you and then continue reading. When you become more aware of the types of interruptions in your efforts to concentrate, you can more quickly refocus your attention.

WHAT IS ATTENTION?

Attention is often referred to as awareness, focus, consciousness, presence of mind. Mastering attention means you are capable of being intentionally focused at will. This greatly improves the quality of your life and your learning. When you are able to open up and hold your attention on something or someone, you tend to listen better, remember more, and take in a richer, deeper experience.

Attention allows you to select and receive information and sensations. When you loose the thread of your attention, sometimes you cannot remember what has just occurred right in front of your eyes and ears. Many accidents and misunderstandings are the direct result of failing attention. A good example of the costly impact of poor attention occurs when you fail to read the fine print of advertisements or sales agreements. Innumerable car accidents occur when the drivers' attention is distracted by electronic devices such as cell phones or musical equipment. How well you can direct and sustain your attention is an essential component of your learning ability and your well-being.

Inner Attention

Attention is more that just watching external events. Attention can be applied to subtle inner experiences. One great example is a mindfulness exercise in meditation that requires you to perform controlled breathing and maintain attention on each breath exhaled. Keeping your attention on your out breath requires the diligent perception of focused attention. With practice, this inwardly attentive technique can be used to still the mind and open yourself to a more receptive and sensitive state. This is exactly where the idea of taking 10 deep breaths comes from. Try it the next time you want to calm your mind. Simply breathe in slowly and fully, then exhale slowly and completely. Keep your attention on the sensation of breathing and nothing else. After doing this 10 times, you may notice a slight shift in your thoughts and body tensions. Try to remember that something as simple as focusing on your breathing can refocus your attention and shift your repetitive thought patterns.

Attention is more than just "what your mind is doing"; it is a combination of the awareness and observation of your inner processes and your external world. In some situations, focusing attention may require that you not think or analyze at all. Instead, it means more fully experiencing your senses by truly seeing what you see and completely hearing what you hear, and being present to both your inner and outer worlds.

As you move your attention to your senses, body, thoughts, and feelings, you become more aware of each of them, gaining a greater insight and understanding of yourself and the world around you. Attention can be used to create something referred to as *meta-awareness*. Meta-awareness is the process of actively observing the content of your awareness. It asks the question, "What am I aware of?"

Attention can be directly used to enhance self-awareness. You can observe your thoughts and actions instead of operating on autopilot. By observing your thoughts and feelings, you slow down automatic reactions and create an opportunity to choose your response. It is like looking at a film or instant replay in slow motion. When you direct your attention consciously toward your thoughts and feelings, they are more clearly revealed.

Attention is our most important tool in the task of improving our experience.

—MIHALY CSIKSZENTMIHALYI

The most powerful aspect of being able to exercise a conscious choice is that you begin to change old or inappropriate habits and thought patterns. The primary barrier to changing negative thought patterns or self-destructive habits is denying that there is a problem. You do this by failing to focus your attention on the need to change. As long as your attention is diverted, you do not have to face the dilemmas of your situations. For example, if someone has a weakness for sweets and it is adversely affecting her health, every time she reaches for the cookies, she must stop paying attention to her health. Before she knows it, and without an awareness, she has eaten an entire bag of cookies—usually while watching TV. It is almost like she lured her attention to focus on the TV so she does not *attend* to what she is eating. Thought patterns are much more difficult to observe. It is possible to have very self-defeating thoughts that you simply take for granted. The boundaries between thoughts, beliefs, and reality are very fine lines. If you are thinking thoughts like "I am never going to finish this college degree," then you are actually building a mental case for why you might fail or drop out. The concept of a self-fulfilling prophesy means you set yourself up for misfortune or success by constantly thinking or talking about it.

The ability to monitor the shifts in your thoughts and bring your attention back to where you are and what you are doing is a key to increasing your comprehension and listening skills. Developing awareness through intentionally focusing your attention is a huge step toward self-mastery.

Student Perspective

SELF-MASTERY AND SELF-AWARENESS

It is not unusual to be sitting in a lecture listening attentively when all of a sudden the lyrics to that new song pop into your head. In an instant, you are no longer in class; rather, you are sitting in some mental void trying to remember the last three words in the second verse. It is bad enough that you drifted off and are now missing the whole lecture, but it is even worse that you haven't realized the shift in your thoughts. These shifts of attention come and go so naturally and effortlessly for most people that minutes (or longer) can pass before they notice. The development of meta-awareness, an ability to consciously stay connected to what it is you are thinking about, can mean the difference between hearing what's on the exam or missing it entirely. It can be the difference between learning a shortcut method to solve a complex equation or missing it and having to struggle with long calculations.

If you regularly practice this sort of mental "check-in" to observe what your attention is focused on and become comfortable with these checks, then automatic drifting is greatly reduced. These "check-ins" allow you to see that your focus has shifted so that you can get your attention back on track more quickly and effectively—before you miss important information.

REFLECTION QUESTIONS

Recall a situation when you experienced this sort of mental drifting during a time that you should have been actively paying attention. This could be in a class or during a reading assignment or a test. How long did it take for you to realize you had lost your focus? Did you lose track of both time and your focus? What was the result of losing control of your attention?

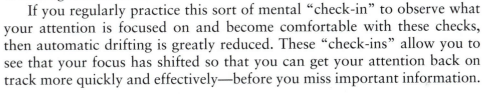

Selective Attention

We live in a culture that is brimming with visual, auditory, and informational overload. Perceptually, we can only attend to a limited amount of stimulus or information before we become mentally confused or emotionally frustrated. In many workplace situations, we must screen out noise, visual distractions, side conversations, and physical discomforts to complete a task. The ability to stay focused and keep our cool on the job are key assets to employee integrity. Our busy lifestyles are also predisposed to innumerable distractions and demands on our attention. You may notice that there are certain times of day when your attention is so scattered you are likely to make poor decisions or become forgetful.

The ability to selectively direct your attention at will, in the midst of extreme distractions, is not a natural, effortless occurrence; it is a skill. Focused inner attention is a mastery that is taught in many martial art forms. Practitioners are often trained to hold their attention on the place just below the navel, which is assumed to be the seat of inner power or "chi." During competitive martial art matches, the slightest wavering of inner focus can go to the opponent's advantage. This is true in almost any competitive sport. Attention is the key to bringing your full potential to bear on any situation.

An emotionally motivated interest can often be a great asset in maintaining your attention. For example, if you enjoy golf, it is much easier to maintain your concentration than if you are trying to read an algebra chapter that you feel is uninspiring. When you are emotionally connected to something, it feels quite easy to stay focused on it; for example, the feeling of love gives you boundless energy and inspiration with which to sustain your attention on the object of your passion. Because you cannot rely on maintaining a consistently high emotional interest in everything, some form of practice geared to fine-tune and strengthen your focus is usually necessary. If no efforts are made to train your ability to focus, you may have attention spans so limited that you are unable to learn efficiently.

Attention can be compared to the beam of a flashlight in an otherwise dark room. Wherever you place the beam of light, you can better see the objects in the room as well as their attributes such as size, color, and relationship to other objects. Your attention is the *perceiving* and *receiving* aspect of your mind. As you move your attention to the outer world, you begin to consciously or unconsciously select what you perceive and how much you take in. If your attention is trained to stay focused in the face of distractions, its span grows wider and longer. Instead of being like a flashlight beam in a dark room, finely tuned attention is like turning on all of the lights in the entire house. The trick is that your mind cannot take in all of the detail of the entire house at once without blowing a fuse!

Selective attention brings to the forefront of your awareness only a small fraction of the perceivable stimulus. It is a natural process that protects you from overload; however, it can also cause you to miss important cues or information vital to your learning or decision-making process. When you can choose the objects of your perception instead of allowing your rambling and random thoughts to select the stimulus, you are able to concentrate. Concentration is attention that is intentionally focused.

Try This

THE TRICK OF SELECTIVE ATTENTION

See if you can figure out the selective perception that this card trick is counting on to befuddle the audience. Look carefully at the cards and *pick one.* Hold the image of your card in your mind. Through the magic of timeless and distant psychic powers, I will now read your mind and remove the card you are thinking of from the card display. Focus and think of nothing but your card; visualize it so it can be seen in your minds' eye. Remember how your card looks and quickly turn to page 73 to see whether your card has been removed.

For Your Journal

SYMBOLS AND ATTENTION

*Please respond to the following in your journal or by using the **Journal Module** on the* CW.

In this book, several *recurring symbols,* or *icons,* are used to call attention to certain activities or content.

Now, create a recurring symbol of your own. Select a special item—a coin, a smooth stone, a special pen, or a piece of jewelry—and place it somewhere in your daily environment, or in your pocket or purse, as a wake-up reminder for your attention. When you come across this item, make a sincere attempt to stop thinking about whatever you are thinking. Literally stop, stand still, and make the mental space necessary to refocus your attention. Use your vision as an indicator that your are refocused. If you can see what you are looking at with greater clarity and detail, it is a good indicator that you have successfully refocused your attention. Try to notice any other shifts in your posture or feelings that refocusing your attention on this object may create.

PAY ATTENTION!

As often as this phrase, *pay attention,* has been used, few people are aware of the actual costs involved in expending your attention. Have you ever wondered what you are paying for your attention *with?*

You pay for your attention with your energy and time. In this context, energy is defined as any expenditure of yourself. What you place your attention on has huge repercussions in your life. In some ways, attention is the force that creates the direction of your life because what you consistently pay attention to is given greater value or importance.

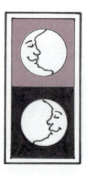

For Your Journal

Companion
Website

ATTENTION AND ENERGY

Please respond to the following in your journal or by using the Journal Module on the CW.

Noticing what catches your attention tells you volumes about your values, interests, preferences, and fears. See if you can find a personal example for each of these statements:

- Where your attention goes, your energy usually follows. *Example: After watching a fast-paced movie I feel exhausted.*

- Where your energy goes, your attention follows. *Example: While working out at the gym I was very aware of how out of shape I had gotten.*

- Events that shape your realities only exist in your consciousness when you bring them into your awareness through your attention. *Example: When I watch the news I become more aware of the struggles of other nations.*

EFFORTLESS ATTENTION

Your interest level is a factor that greatly impacts how attentive you are. When your interest level is low, your attention may seem to have a will of its own. A classic example occurs when you are sitting in class trying to listen to a lecture on your least favorite subject and you find your attention has wandered off on its own private adventure. Yet, when you watch a movie or TV program you enjoy, you easily attend to it without effort and can often recall the entire show in great detail. What is the nature of these differences in how you are capable of concentrating?

TV, movies, and even the Internet require very little intentional attention from viewers. Programs, commercials, and feature films are devised to demand nominal attention spans. Using special effects and visually engaging formats, media producers and advertisers are always creating new ways to get, and keep, your attention. What you view on the screen can be so vivid that it actually appears realer than real. You can be almost hypnotized by the magnificent visuals. All this requires is an effortless or mindless cooperation from an audience. In this passive state, you can stay entranced for hours. Although trances can be highly receptive states, they may disconnect you from your personal goals and values and insert those of the advertiser or movie maker. In the long run, you can probably imagine some of the potential dangers to an entire culture that is hypnotized by this type of media. On the other hand, classroom presentations are rarely as visually compelling and captivating as a Spielberg film or a good football game. This is exactly why *you must manage your attention* if you value education and learning.

Student Perspective

ACTIVELY ATTENDING AND OBSERVING THE DETAILS

It happens every semester—you walk into class and see the dreaded overhead transparency machine. Maybe there is a slide projector or a TV and VCR in the corner. Even if these things are not present, there is always a huge wall-sized chalkboard or whiteboard on which the professor will no doubt be scrawling truckloads of information. For those students with more visual learning styles, this may be wonderful, but in many cases, it means you are required to copy down information, diagrams, formulas, and other materials during class. This presents an interesting question: How do you listen to what is being said, take notes, copy what is on the board, and actually absorb anything during a one-hour class period?

The good news is that whatever is shown visually is usually related to what is being discussed, so you won't really be stretched in too many directions. Your task is to organize and plan your approach and have a clear feel for what is really important. Some visual aids are used as supplemental material for whatever is being discussed, so it is very natural to integrate the pictures with the notes. Other visual aids might be copies of material in your textbook and may not have to be copied into your notes. Some material may be very important and show up on the next exam—so you had better not only copy it down, but also do it accurately! When in doubt as to exactly what your professor intends when using visual aids, don't hesitate to ask. It is not wrong to ask, "Should I copy this down?" Most professors will tell you how you should approach the material. If it turns out that the visual aids are important aspects of the lesson material, make sure that you get them copied and that you fully understand their relevance to the lesson. This means that you must pay attention to what the professor is saying while directing your focus on the details of what you are seeing. This is not always easy, but with practice and conscious effort, it is a very powerful learning tool.

Some helpful pointers: Look carefully and completely at what is being shown so you can copy it accurately. Be prepared to inquire about aspects you don't understand. If you are at all uncertain, ask your professor to explain or clarify the visual aid. If you don't know what certain symbols or icons stand for, ask about them. If you can't read something, ask (not all professors have great handwriting). If the professor is moving through the material more quickly than you can write, politely ask him or her to slow down. If you sit in the back of the room and can hardly see, move up closer.

REFLECTION QUESTIONS

Are visual aids a help or hindrance to your learning process in the classroom? When are they used effectively? How can they be used ineffectively?

Flow

A form of effortless attention that works in alignment with your values is known as *flow* or *optimal experience*. Flow occurs when you are doing something you love. What you are doing may require effort and energy, but your attention flows naturally and willingly. In his book called *Flow* (1990), Mihaly Csikszentmihalyi suggests that the best moments of an optimal experience occur "when a person's body or mind is stretched to its limits in a voluntary effort to accomplish something difficult and worthwhile" (p. 3). Staying true to your purpose or passion creates a quality of attention that is felt as enjoyment and exhilaration.

If you are not interested in something, it is difficult if not impossible to keep your attention focused. Discovering what distracts or sustains your attention provides powerful insights into how you can open up your learning process and life experience to deeper levels. Let's start by examining a few of the distracting situations that affect the quality of energy necessary to focus your attention.

Outward Distracters

Outward distracters are *uncomfortable or unusual environmental situations, including noises, lighting, chaotic movement, or other overwhelming sensual input*. Outward distracters are sometimes more easily resolved than those that are inward. When the lighting is bad, you can change it or move to another location. Likewise, when the noise level interferes with your thinking, you can usually find an area that is quieter. Whenever possible, do your best to resolve or avoid outward distracters before you attempt to concentrate your attention. One solution is to arrange for a place with minimal distractions in your daily environment. Use your self-awareness to note when you are too distracted to concentrate. Stop struggling with the distractions—before you get frustrated or lose interest, find a reasonable place of retreat where you can use your energy to focus.

Often, students are required to work or study in places with a high number of distractions. Even a library can be buzzing with people and ambient background sounds that are annoying. The workplace typically is not a sanctuary of peace and solitude either. We all have varying levels of tolerance for distractions and must know when to apply our skills and efforts to sustain and focus our attention. Using the power of our attention to concentrate in spite of outer stimuli is a necessary talent because sometimes it is just not possible to retreat or find a less distracting environment.

Inward Distracters

Inward distracters are physiological and psychological concerns that draw on your attention. *Physiological distracters* like hunger, illness, sleepiness, and physical pain can take all of your energy and many times draw on your reserves of patience as well. When your sense of physical well-being is out of balance, your whole attention tends to move toward resolving or avoiding the discomfort.

We have all experienced the draining feeling that occurs when we attempt to stay focused while sleepy or hungry. Battling physiological distracters requires you to be proactive and take preventative measures to minimize or eliminate them before attempting to focus your attention for any extended time. When hungry, eat; when tired, rest. Chapter 4 discusses the connections between sleep, nutrition, stress, and exercise and a person's energy level and sense of well-being. Review these topics for tips on building the physical energy reserves necessary to keep your attention sharp and clear.

Psychological distractions include thoughts and emotions. These distractions are sometimes the most challenging because students are rarely trained on how to manage these demanding, and often unconscious, internal voices that tug at their attempts to stay focused.

Emotions take energy, and although you should not disregard your feelings, your awareness of *how much attention you give them* gives you the ability to choose the intensity of the emotion. When you realize that you are "fueling the fire" of your emotions with your thinking process, then you can decide whether keeping your attention on intensified emotions will be more valuable to your well-being than moving your attention back to the tasks or situations in your present external environment. For example, if you are upset with your partner, you cannot afford to keep thinking about the argument and increasing your emotional turmoil if you wish to focus on doing well on a test.

Extreme emotional states can cause your attention to become stuck—you find yourself in a repetitive loop where your heightened feelings create thought patterns that verge on obsession. You cannot seem to "stop thinking" about an event or situation that occurred in the past or might occur in the future. Extreme emotional states can be positive or negative. You have probably noticed that it is just as difficult to maintain attention when overly excited as it is when upset or frustrated.

Present-minded thinking is a state of neutral, nonjudgmental observation. When you are ruled by highly emotional thoughts, you tend to lose ground. Sometimes, you can be consumed by thoughts that dwell on the past or fears about the future. Keeping your attention *in the present* can liberate you from the powerful grip of energy-draining emotionality.

Try This

LETTING NEGATIVE EMOTIONS GO

When you find yourself dwelling on an upsetting situation or worrying about some future problem, try this technique. As worrisome thoughts arise, refocus your attention on one thing you are grateful for. Keep your attention on this feeling of gratitude for a least a minute and inwardly verbalize why you are thankful. Watch how relentless the worrisome thought will be. As it tries again to surface, repeat and acknowledge your gratitude with even more sincere resolve. What you are observing is a small inner battlefield. Decide who you really want to win—the worrisome thoughts or the gratitude. Keep at it. You will notice that the worrisome thoughts retreat if your resolve to replace them with positive emotions is strong.

ATTENTION AND STRESSFUL STATES OF MIND

In his book *Emotional Intelligence* (1997), Daniel Goleman describes what he calls "attentional stance under duress" (p. 49). Goleman found that when people are faced with extremely distressful situations, there are two distinct responses. One group of people became vigilant, able to focus attention on the details of the predicament. The other group's reaction to distress was avoidance, using their attention to distract themselves from the stressful event. Goleman notes that these two contrasting responses indicate the intensity with which people experience emotions. Those who felt more intensely tended to choose avoidance; those who could detach emotionally stayed powerfully focused. Impatience, confusion, and anxiety are stressful states of mind that can create the avoidance response. This could explain why we so often find ourselves participating in distracting activities.

Boredom and impatience are two very distracting emotional states. When bored, we resist giving our attention to people or situations. Our attention level can become so low that we actually feel sleepy or become frustrated in an unconscious attempt to avoid further contact with the situation. When we are impatient we may get irritable. Irritability often turns into blaming someone or something, and blame can distract us from accurately assessing a situation.

Confusion is an inner state that quickly disperses all of the energy needed for attention. Indecision is often a result of confusion. We begin to feel like we are spinning our wheels or sinking in quicksand when overwhelmed with information or emotional input. Our attention becomes extremely fatigued and fragmented, limiting our focusing abilities. Thoughts flood in so fast, we start to lose clarity and purpose. This can result in our inability to make a decision or take a necessary action.

Anxiety and depression can also cycle around with confusion and indecision. In our culture, the stressful lifestyles have created an epidemic of depression and anxiety-related problems. Empowering yourself to refocus your attention on positive, peaceful, and relaxing impressions can relieve you of the grip of many types of stress and anxiety.

For Your Journal

PRACTICING VISUALIZATION

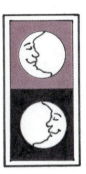

*Please respond to the following in your journal or by using the **Journal Module** on the CW.*

Practice this stress-reduction technique and write about your experience. First, locate a place where you can be undisturbed for about 10 minutes. Take stock of the tension in your body. Notice the areas that are tight or constricted. Now, close your eyes and take yourself on a mental vacation. Recall a relaxing setting. Now, immerse yourself in the sensations of the setting. Recall the sounds, sights, and smells and bring them into a vivid presence in your mind's eye. Briefly return your attention to the areas of tension and invite them to relax with you. When you return from your break, write about any noticeable changes in your emotional state.

INTENTIONAL FOCUSED ATTENTION

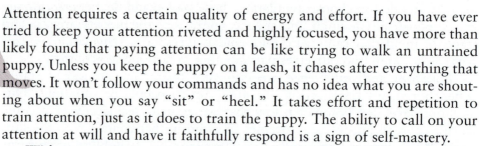

Attention requires a certain quality of energy and effort. If you have ever tried to keep your attention riveted and highly focused, you have more than likely found that paying attention can be like trying to walk an untrained puppy. Unless you keep the puppy on a leash, it chases after everything that moves. It won't follow your commands and has no idea what you are shouting about when you say "sit" or "heel." It takes effort and repetition to train attention, just as it does to train the puppy. The ability to call on your attention at will and have it faithfully respond is a sign of self-mastery.

Without a purpose, your attention remains aimless. Perhaps that is obvious. There is no reason to train your attention if you have no idea what you want it to do. There is an old Zen parable that claims that if you could be diligently single-minded for only an hour and hold one uninterrupted thought, you could manifest whatever it was you focused on. In other words, the parable suggests that the power of being able to hold attention in this manner and duration would be intense enough to create something right out of thin air. According to the story, this is never possible because no matter how strongly you wish for something, your attention will not stay where you direct it to go for any length of time.

Attention does improve with practice, and there are methods of growing attention. Just like working out to build a muscle, certain practices can strengthen attention.

Methods for Strengthening Attention

The following are some suggestions for strengthening your attention:

- *Clarify an aim for your attention.* Ask yourself, "What is it I want to attend to?" If your aim is to keep your attention on listening to a lecture, then if you are no longer hearing and understanding the words, you know you have missed your target. With an aim in mind, you can quickly refocus and stay on course.

- *Connect your values and goals to how you direct your attention.* How does focusing your attention on this aim serve your values and goals? If it does not serve your values, then question why you have chosen to expend your attention on something that is not in alignment with your values or principles.

- *Check your posture.* A straight spine is important to alertness. There is a great deal of wisdom underlying the military's emphasis on standing at attention. The erect spine allows the body to be in an alert and open state.

Martial arts practitioners assume an erect posture where all of the muscles are completely free of tension. There is an advantage to not expending energy on unnecessary bodily tension—that energy is then freed up to use in directing your attention. Check your posture and body tensions—keep your spine straight and your body relaxed to maximize your focusing ability.

■ *Breathe!* In yoga, many postures are designed to open and align the spine as well as expand the volume of breathing. This allows more oxygen to the lungs, increasing the brain's physiological ability to be more alert and attentive.

■ *Split your attention. Grounding* is a method of being present in your physical body. It requires a relaxed, soft focus between an inner observation of your mind and an active sensation of some aspect of your body. Grounding your attention on your body is like putting your mind or emotions in neutral. For example, when you are aware of the sensation of your breathing, this type of attention helps you shift perspective. It is especially useful if you are stuck in a negative emotion or an unproductive thought pattern.

A key to grounding your attention is to split your awareness—50 percent on observation of the external environment and 50 percent on observation of your internal state, including your emotions and thoughts. Neither aspect is more important than the other because it is the synthesis of these two mental areas (internal and external) that allows you to internalize, thus remember, the stimulus you take in.

Use grounding when you have to shift gears or come back to yourself. From a neutral perspective, you can better choose where you wish to refocus your attention. This balancing of your inner attention with the outer world can reduce stressful thoughts and emotions as well as bring renewed energy to the process of focusing your attention.

■ *Be mindful.* In a mindful state, you slow down your thoughts, taking greater care to inwardly observe, sense, and feel—you become more sensitive to yourself and others. The scope of perception is wider, but you can also grasp vivid detail. Mindfulness can be used to deal with boredom by returning to the "beginner's mind." It is easy to be bored if you feel there is nothing new to be gained or learned. When you return to the "beginner's mind," you treat all information and situations as if they are occurring for the first time. This inner attitude keeps you fresh and allows you to gain insight and new perspectives. It ends the negative inner talk that says, "Been there, done that" or "I've heard all of this before." Instead, as you see things anew, you also notice subtleties or aspects that you may have missed. Because the beginner's mind is empty and receptive, it is highly capable of attending to new information.

What If . . .

What if your memory could be strengthened to recall everything you read and hear in photographic detail? When your attention is focused and you use your observation skills, you register what your senses of sight and sound perceive. Without accurate observation, you only remember fragments and your comprehension is compromised.

ACTIVE LISTENING AND ACCURATE OBSERVATION

The difference between listening and hearing is that when you actively listen, you begin to understand. *Active listening* requires more than just hearing the words spoken. It means asking questions, restating what was said, and giving feedback to the speaker. Most people listen with only part of their attention. While the other person is still speaking, we are thinking about what we want to say next, or sometimes we are thinking of something entirely unrelated to the conversation. To stay actively engaged in the listening process, try *subvocalization,* which is the process of "speaking" each word you hear to yourself. Bringing your attention fully to the words you are hearing by restating them internally helps you remember and retain what is said. You can also practice splitting your attention by framing a question or comment to offer the speaker while continuing to actively listen. Active listening requires your full engagement.

Accurate observation involves more than simply taking in the visual stimulus around you; it requires your active participation in your visual observations. Simply "seeing" something is not the same as "accurately observing" it; attention must be intentionally focused and controlled in order to truly observe with accuracy. It is interesting to note that eyewitness accounts of a crime are considered the most unreliable form of evidence. Most people who observe an occurrence are simply "seeing"—not making an intentional effort to accurately observe. Therefore, their observations are often faulty and unreliable. To avoid this pitfall, you must make the effort to focus your attention and consciously choose to dissect or analyze what you are seeing. Choosing to observe the similarities, differences, colors, patterns, or other attributes of a visual stimulus offers greater comprehension and more accurate observation. It is also important to use objectivity, rather than assumptions, when observing because believing is not always seeing. It is easy to miss details and important aspects of what you see when your focus is not directed in an objective manner.

DISTRACTER	SUSTAINER
Poor health	Good nutrition, exercise, and rest
Unusual or uncomfortable environmental situations	Change the setting or arrange for a comfortable setting
Physical discomforts	Resolve them before trying to attend
Extreme emotional states	Grounding with attention to sensation of the body
Stress and anxiety	Straighten spine, relax muscles, and breathe intentionally
Boredom	Clarify an aim connected to values or goals
Confusion	Stop fragmented thinking by refocusing on a physical activity

Distracters and sustainers.   **TABLE 3.1**

Try This

TAPPING INTO ATTENTION

What is your experience of attention? To get a personal sense of grounding and the movement and duration of your personal attention span, try this exercise. Sit quietly and make an effort to clear your mind. Try to stop thinking completely. Focus in on the sensation of your left foot. Tap your foot slowly and lightly. How does your foot feel in your shoe? Is it hot, cold, cramped, pulsating? Do your best to notice all of the sensations of your toes, the sole of your foot, your ankle. Keep your attention on your left foot for as long as you can—at least several minutes. Before long, you should notice that your attention is on the move. The object of this exercise is to *notice the exact moment your attention starts to move* away from focusing on your left foot.

For the next five minutes, go back to focusing on the sensations of your left foot by softly tapping and continue to watch for the moment that your attention makes its move. You will probably observe that your attention moves much faster than you can think about it. Make a mental note of what the movement of your attention *feels like.* You may notice a thought that gives your attention permission to move. For example, your inner voice may say, "This exercise is not important" or "You have done this long enough." Watch how those thoughts attempt to take over, but don't let them.

As you become more observant of and familiar with the feeling of your attention as it moves, you can begin to extend the span and duration of your focus. This exercise will help you learn *the feeling of your attention going out of focus.* Little by little, you will begin to catch your attention as it is moving and you will be able to keep your focus for a longer duration. As with most things, this exercise works best if you use it often.

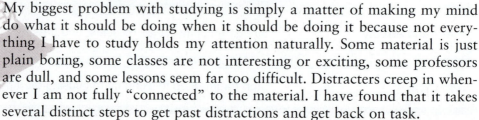

Student Perspective

DEALING WITH DISTRACTIONS

My biggest problem with studying is simply a matter of making my mind do what it should be doing when it should be doing it because not everything I have to study holds my attention naturally. Some material is just plain boring, some classes are not interesting or exciting, some professors are dull, and some lessons seem far too difficult. Distracters creep in whenever I am not fully "connected" to the material. I have found that it takes several distinct steps to get past distractions and get back on task.

First, I have to recognize that the distraction exists. In order to overcome a distraction, I must notice it is there and identify it as something that is causing my attention to slip. This might sound simple (and even a little silly), but it is easy to simply ignore or overlook the external or internal things that might be interfering with my ability to focus. That dripping tap water or song in my mind may be more problematic than I might first believe. I may be more tired than I thought or have things on my mind that I didn't notice. Staying in touch with myself through my self-awareness helps me identify any distractions that may be lurking.

The second step is to accept the fact that my attention has slipped. Making the conscious acknowledgment that I am "off task" helps to bring me back into the area of refocusing my attention. I admit to myself that I have lost my focus as soon as I have identified the distracter or cause, and I reaffirm to myself that it is OK. This brings me one step closer to resolving the problem. Over time, and with consistent effort, dealing with distractions became second nature because I now know exactly what my personal signals are without giving it too much thought.

Finally, I resolve to eliminate the distracter or remove myself from it and refocus my attention. This is tough because some things are not easily controlled. I cannot, for example, stop the person behind me from sniffling all the way through a chemistry lecture or make a faulty lightbulb stop flickering while I'm trying to watch a slide show presentation. By eliminating it, I don't mean "make it stop" as much as I mean "move past it."

This resolution varies with the type of distraction I am facing and the specific situation I am in. Some distractions are very powerful, or even totally out of my control, but by acknowledging and accepting their presence, I can move right past the distraction and get back on task. It is my mind, after all—I can exercise the right to redirect it back to wherever I choose. Of course, this is a skill that I had to develop, but it was more than worth the effort if I consider everything gained from staying focused. I have put a great deal of time, money, and effort into my education, and I am not about to let a few little distractions get in my way!

REFLECTION QUESTIONS

What are some of your most challenging distractions? Discuss some of your methods for dealing with them.

SUMMARY

This chapter has addressed the importance of **attention** as a key to learning, and how you, as an active participant in the learning process, must practice ways to train your attention. You have examined various types of **distracters** that might impede your ability to focus. This connection between your attention and your ability to gain and retain information can be applied by **active listening** and **accurate observation.**

Attention is more than simply "watching" or "listening"; it is a complex mental and sensual process that requires active participation. You must accept responsibility for actively choosing what you focus on.

A **distraction** is anything that interrupts your focus. Distractions come from the outside environment or from inside oneself.

Some outward distracters that were discussed include:

- noise
- lighting
- temperature
- other people

Some of the inward distracters you looked at are:

- physiological distractions such as hunger, fatigue, and illness
- psychological distractions such as thoughts and emotions

Each person has an individual level of tolerance for distractions and must develop methods to overcome them. The key lies in finding those tools and techniques that allow you to gain control over and direct your focus at will. Some suggestions for overcoming distractions include **mindfulness,** the art of maintaining an awareness of what you are seeing, hearing, and feeling from moment to moment. **Grounding** is the practice of splitting your attention between an awareness of the sensation of your body and observation of your thoughts.

Active listening refers to your ability to stay connected and in control of what you hear in a way that helps you retain information and fully understand. **Accurate observation** is a technique that involves consciously taking in detailed information in such a way that you are certain of the correctness of what you have seen.

You can learn to acknowledge and respond to your own personal cues of attention, to know when your focus has been lost, to identify any distracters you are facing, and then to refocus your attention on what you want to attend to. This requires learning to exercise vigilant **self-awareness** and learning to balance your attention on both your inner and outer environments.

Case Studies

CASE STUDY 3.1

Prioritizing and Selective Attention

Jamaal was just promoted to assistant manager. Along with a healthy increase in pay, this promotion also includes an increase in Jamaal's responsibilities. The new position requires him to be in charge of loss management and theft prevention. He is now responsible for ensuring that his coworkers are charging the correct prices for all sales items, that the deliveries the store receives are all accurate, and that there is no theft of any kind occurring in the store. These tasks require that Jamaal pay attention to what is going on in the store at all times. Any lapse in his attention could mean that items get stolen or end up missing. Because Jamaal will be held responsible for any item stolen, it is very important that he makes sure things are correctly observed and that he stays focused.

You are the store manager in this scenario. You are now holding a meeting to discuss the training methods that will be used to prepare Jamaal for his duties.

The skill set listed below is the foundation for Jamaal's new responsibilities:

- Accurate observation of sales staff and customers

- Accurate observation and attention to detail regarding stock deliveries
- Active listening
- Dealing with distractions

What specific training and advice regarding inner and outer distractors will you give Jamaal to prepare him to successfully fulfill these responsibilities?

CASE STUDY 3.2
Time Management and Attention

Cinda has less than 48 hours to prepare for her biology midterm. She is generally a good student; in fact she is holding a high B in the course. If she aces the midterm, she could easily move to a solid A. Cinda plans to major in environmental sciences. She is passionately interested in preserving and protecting natural environments. Yet, like a bad action movie, she is procrastinating—doing everything but the research necessary to prepare for the essay on the exam. Follow along and notice all of the twists and turns of Cinda's attention as she makes a valiant attempt to impose order in a world of endless distractions.

As the clock ticks away, Cinda sits down to the computer with a plan of focusing on her research. As soon as she goes on-line, her friend Sharla pops up and asks if she would like to chat. Cinda takes a few minutes to vent to Sharla about her overwhelmingly busy day at work. By now, it is 7:30 at night, and Cinda realizes that her day was so busy that she forgot to eat. She signs off with Sharla and jumps up to make a snack. Remembering that she should check the weather for the next day before setting out her clothes for the morning, Cinda flips through the TV channels while eating her snack. She watches a few minutes of the weather forecast. Then, she flips the remote to a rerun channel and while mindlessly watching *I Love Lucy,* she begins thinking about how rudely a customer treated her. Her inner dialog kicks in, and she finds she is now imagining giving the customer a piece of her mind. Then, she recalls how she was written up on another job last year for "inappropriate language." She tells herself that the boss was so unsupportive she is still glad she quit working there. Now, she can't stop thinking about what a poorly trained supervisor she has at her current job. Before she realizes it, another hour has passed. Cinda starts to feel uncontrollably tired. It is after 9:30 and she is getting way too sleepy to do any research tonight. Even though she is feeling increasingly stressed about having only a few hours tomorrow to do the research, she decides to take a shower and get some rest.

When Cinda wakes up the next morning, she realizes that she slept poorly. She has a pounding headache and discovers that she forgot to set the alarm. This means that both she and her friend are going to be late for class.

REFLECTION QUESTIONS

1. Write the rest of this scenario for Cinda. What will most likely occur during Cinda's day if she continues on the "path of no attention"? What will happen to her efforts to focus on the research for the midterm?

2. Can you identify the places where Cinda was responsible for creating her own distractions?

3. What advice would you offer Cinda to help her focus her attention?

CASE STUDY 3.3

Attention Deficit

When a Web search for the word "attention" was done, the top 25 hits were sites related to ADD/ADHD. Review several Internet sites that offer information (not products) on ADD (attention deficit disorder). Once you have reviewed the on-line background information on ADD, read the following scenario.

You are an instructor at a community college. You have recently completed a training seminar designed to help teachers identify adult ADD students. In the seminar, you learned that approximately 10 percent of students have some degree of ADD. Of that 10 percent, only 3 percent are aware they have this condition, and only 1 percent are registered with the college learning differences program.

After a careful observation of student homework, test scores, and classroom interaction, you believe you have identified three students in your class who might have ADD. Another student has already informed you privately that he has ADD. The college program for students with learning differences arranges for this student, who has been formally diagnosed, to have alternative testing arrangements where he is allowed more time. The other three students, who appear to have ADD but have not been formally diagnosed, do not get this benefit and are failing the course.

As the instructor, how do you handle this? Should you discuss your concerns with the students? Or is it their responsibility to figure out why they are not doing well in college? What do you see as the role of the education system to assist adult students with ADD?

Demonstration of Competency

*Please respond to the following in your journal or by using the **Demonstration of Competency Module** on the CW.*

Rate your competency for the concepts listed below using this scale:

1 = no experiences or ideas   2 = a few ideas but no experience   3 = some experience
4 = I know all I need to know about this   5 = I am an expert

CONCEPT	RATING
Effortless attention	
Selective attention	
Intentionally focused attention	

Set a personal learning objective for any concept that you rated as 1 or 2. Write a sentence stating what you will commit to do and how you plan to learn more about the concept during the next week.

_____

_____

_____

_____

_____

Refer to your notes from the exercise on Attention Accounting on pages 50–51. What was the nature of your most persistent distraction in this exercise? What skills might help you minimize this type of distraction? Describe how the distractions while reading relate to your potential success as a student or employee.

_____

_____

_____

_____

_____

Define these concepts in terms of your own experience.

ATTENTION

_____

_____

_____

EFFORTLESS ATTENTION

_____

_____

_____

SELECTIVE ATTENTION

_____

_____

_____

OUTWARD DISTRACTERS

_____

_____

_____

INWARD DISTRACTERS

_____

_____

_____

INTENTIONAL ATTENTION

_____

_____

_____

Answer to the Card Trick

Look! I have read your mind and taken away the card you were thinking of!

Now, without looking back to page 55, see if you can figure out the role of selective attention in this card trick.

Additional references and resources for chapter topics can be found at **www.prenhall.com/gray**

Energy

MENTAL AND PHYSICAL WELL-BEING

The art of resting the mind and the power of dismissing from it all care and worry is probably one of the secrets of energy in all great [people].

—J. A. HADFIELD

In this chapter, you will consider the connections between clarity, well-being, and the energy needed to enhance the quality of life. By using a series of self-assessments and your sense of vital energy as a barometer, you will create methods to keep your mental and physical health in balance. You will explore methods of self-awareness that can reestablish a connection to your own innate ability to maintain and cultivate well-being.

What If . . .

What if you woke up each morning feeling refreshed, relaxed, and energized? Do you feel strong, comfortable, and clear headed? Think of a few words or phrases that describe how you might feel and perform if you are in the prime of health.

DEFINING OPTIMAL HEALTH

Defining your attributes for optimal health is the first step in creating a measurement to gauge what gives you energy and what detracts from it. Knowing the subtleties of your own sense of vitality can provide you with early warning clues to when you are becoming toxic, imbalanced, or depleted. Making health decisions that give you a better quality of life begins with your clarity about what provides you with good energy.

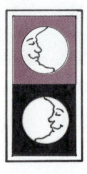

For Your Journal

Companion
Website

SETTING THE BAR FOR OPTIMAL HEALTH

Please respond to the following in your journal or by using the **Journal Module** *on the CW.*

In this journal exercise, you will be describing your ideal *feeling* of vitality and well-being. Whenever possible, relate these feelings to your own experiences and examples. Try using the starter sentences below if you are not sure how to begin your descriptions.

When I am feeling healthy, my body is

_____

_____

Vitality means my strength is

_____

_____

Well-being is a state of

_____

_____

I feel energetic when I

_____

_____

Now, online or on a separate sheet, summarize in a few paragraphs what optimal health feels like for you. Make sure to use plenty of descriptive words.

WHAT IS ENERGY?

Energy in the context of personal health can be a nebulous term. In traditional world cultures, it is called such names as *Mana* in Polynesia, *Prana* in India, *Qi* in China, *Ki* in Japan, and *Hucha* and *Sami* in Peru. Modern alternative healing techniques refer to it as biofield, life-force energy, physioemotional field, body energy field, vital energies, and subtle energies. For purposes of our exploration of energy, you will *focus on the relationships between your energy levels and your ability to maintain physical well-being and mental clarity.* You will also identify what creates a state of optimal health for you. For example, if having a sense of vitality means feeling relaxed, strong, and resilient, then you might qualify this feeling as a state of high energy. Or if you identify feeling energetic as being focused, productive, or creative, then when you participate in activities of this nature, you could say you are thriving on good energy.

It is equally important to note what drains your energy. Ill health, negative emotional states, or toxicity can sap your energy and push you into overdrive, fatigue, or states of severe imbalance. As you move through the following series of self-assessments, consider what kinds of situations create fluctuations in your energy levels and attempt to make a conscious effort to balance your well-being.

GATHERING ENERGY

If you are in generally good health, you begin each day with fresh and renewed energy. Some of the ordinary rituals you perform daily to gather your energy include eating, bathing, sleeping, and amusing yourself with electronic media, games, hobbies, exercise, and social contact. You nurture yourself with activities that are pleasurable, familiar, beneficial, and comforting. You may not think about how something as simple as your physical contact with a beloved pet can uplift your energy level, but when that contact is absent, you notice a slight depression or sense that something is missing.

You can subconsciously raise your energy with innumerable sensual impressions—from extending your gaze on a dramatic sunset to deeply breathing the subtle fragrance of flowers. These pleasing sensual impressions literally feed your energy level and offset or balance the barrage of energy-draining situations and scenarios you encounter each day. You can invigorate your body and mind through movements and postures that generate more oxygen to your system and reduce tension. For example, even a brisk 20-minute walk or a series of simple yoga stretching exercises can provide a sense of renewal and freshness of mind.

It should be mentioned that too much of a good thing can also throw your vitality for a loop. Energy created by "quick-fix" boosters such as sugar, nicotine, and caffeine can have backlash effects over time. It only takes one "caffeine headache" to be convinced that you are caught in a loop where you can't live with it or without it. Notice that the markets are now carrying a section for "energy drinks." Society's challenging lifestyles make these types of energy enhancers increasingly necessary. Herbal remedies and pharmaceuticals are also commonly overused in an effort to create more energy or stamina. The danger of habitually using stimulants lies in how you exceed your body's natural limits and reach states of exhaustion and lowered immune systems. When you push your body into overdrive, you will inevitably reach an equally dramatic downside. Many people have been living in the overdrive state for so long they have become chronically out of balance. A chain of events that keeps you trapped in a repetitious state of ill health and disease can emerge from false vitality. Only when you remove the quick-fix boosters from your daily routine can you begin to see the true state of your health.

Calming energy works with your state of mind as well as your state of well-being. You may have already developed methods of relaxing or calming your mind—taking a relaxing hot bath, reading a favorite novel, exercising, or being in nature. Without these alternatives, the quick-fix boosters are all too convenient. It is important to keep a repertoire of calming, relaxing, and reenergizing methods and activities accessible to your daily routine. A key to gathering energy is to allow yourself some downtime; in other words, make time to relax each day. In addition to your working, studying, and family or relationship obligations, set aside a minimum of 30 to 60 minutes a day for YOU!

Student Perspective

HEALTH CONSCIOUS—BALANCING SCHOOL AND WORK

The old saying, "working my way through college" is a reality for many students. Very few have the benefit of the financial support that allows them to focus on only their studies. There is added responsibility and stress levels increase when balancing a 30-hour workweek with a 16-credit hour academic load. Part of the price students pay for "doing it all" is the effect on their health and energy levels. When you have to push yourself in this way, it is necessary that you stay aware of your energy levels and keep yourself healthy. This balancing act is not an easy one.

Suppose you have to get up at 7:30 A.M. to prepare for school. You jump in the shower, get some coffee, maybe eat some breakfast, and rush to arrive on campus in time for that 9:00 class. By about noon, you feel a little tired, so you stop off at the cafeteria for a cup of coffee and a donut or grab an energy drink. You are wide awake for that 12:45 lecture and raring to go when 4:00

rolls around and it is time to head to work. An hour into your shift, you feel your energy slipping away, so on your dinner break, you pour yourself a huge cola with plenty of caffeine in it. This helps you make it to 11:00 P.M. when you get to go home. You then remember that you have homework to do. After debating whether or not to just leave it for morning, you splash some cool water on your face, pour yourself another cup of coffee, and get down to it. You hit the sheets at about 3:00 A.M. Then, the cycle begins again—in four and a half hours! Unfortunately, when the alarm goes off, you are really tired, so you hit the snooze button and accidentally oversleep. So, this morning, you skip breakfast and just grab some coffee on the way to class. By the time 4:00 comes around, you have already consumed three cups of java. You go to work, get home, and repeat the same high-energy cycle over the rest of the week.

This is not a hypothetical situation—it is a reality for many students. Although the details may differ, the fact remains that many students have to sacrifice personal time in order to attend school and hold down a job. You might go a week like this and plan to "catch up" on your sleep over the weekend, but the truth is that you do not "catch up," you only "recover" from the draining effect your schedule has on your physical health. Your moods, mental alertness, and overall state of well-being are adversely affected. Sleeping 12 hours straight on Saturday does not completely repair the damage done all week. If you keep this pace up over the next 14 weeks in order to complete the semester, it is quite likely you will deplete yourself to such a degree that you get sick. The human body simply cannot exist on such a rigorous routine, and depending on the individual, this can even be dangerous to long-term health.

Although it might be necessary to work while going to school, care should be taken to minimize the physical stresses as much as possible. Work only as many hours as necessary for your financial situation; you may discover that you can earn enough money to survive on less work hours per week. Adjust your classload to balance the "up" and "down" times; don't try to carry a huge course load while working if it will cut into your sleep time. Set time aside for the important stuff—eating and sleeping; these activities provide the basic fuels your body needs to sustain itself. Take naps during the day when you can instead of drinking caffeine and sugar; these quick-fix energy boosters are no substitute for rest. Most importantly, stay aware of your physical and mental state and adjust as needed to maintain optimal health and energy levels.

REFLECTION QUESTIONS

Do you, or does someone you know, hold a full-time job while going to school? How are the two balanced? What can be done to improve and optimize your energy and health levels? Do you make time for yourself each day?

For Your Journal

Companion Website

TOP 10 ENERGIZERS

*Please respond to the following in your journal or by using the **Journal Module** on the CW.*

First, make a list of the top 10 ways you can gather energy or reenergize yourself.

Then, develop an energizer vocabulary by writing down the words or phrases that best describe how you feel and act when you are in a high-energy state. Be careful to define the difference between your experience of "high energy" and "overdrive."

Energy Drains

Today's demanding lifestyles can sometimes make us too depleted to reenergize, and we find ourselves caught in a downward spiral. Listing the situations and people that drain your energy probably seems easy and obvious. The nagging supervisor, the long waits in traffic, the incompetent repair technicians, inconsiderate roommates—all seem to rob you of your peace of mind and sanity. Unfortunately, the secret thief of your vitality can be the residual stress, anxiety, and negative thoughts and emotions that result from the situations long after they have actually occurred. You lose sleep, eat poorly, and find yourself stuck in confusion, the most insidious energy drain of all.

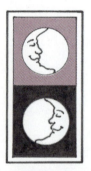

For Your Journal

Companion Website

ENERGY LOSERS

*Please respond to the following in your journal or by using the **Journal Module** on the CW.*

Make a list of the top 10 ways you lose energy.

List the words or phrases that best describe how you feel and act when you are in a low-energy state.

It is estimated that people lose approximately two to three hours a day to indecision, poor decisions, and confusion. The inability to make decisions tends to increase when your energy level is low or unfocused. For example, when you are really hungry, this is often the most difficult time to decide what to eat and is usually when you make the least healthy food choices.

Repetitive negative thoughts and worrying amplify anxiety and stress. Emotional turmoil saps you of energy, and it can take you weeks or months to recover. The downward spiral of low energy usually continues until you hit the bottom. The bottom is typically marked by illness or an unmanageable emotional upset. Stress takes a direct toll on the immune system, making you more susceptible to all manner of ailments. A low-energy attitude can also become as infectious as the common cold. Try observing how differently the world seems to respond to you if you are in a low- or negative-energy state. It may feel like there is literally a dark cloud following you around.

A lack of nutritious food, dehydration, air toxins, allergies, low-grade infections, viruses, colds, and general aches and pains also drain energy. There may be cycles or patterns to your low energy states. For example, certain times of day can be less energetic than others. Early afternoon is a common time of reduced energy. The weather can affect how sleepy or energetic you feel. The most important measure of your energy level comes from your own accounting of subtle changes on a daily basis. The following self-assessment exercise accounts for the top 10 energy losers in your day-to-day life.

For Your Journal

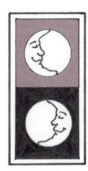

ENERGY MONITOR

*Please respond to the following in your journal or by using the **Journal Module** on the CW.*

This journal exercise requires you to note your energy level throughout the day and evening. Be prepared to recognize subtle changes in your energy that may be indicated by a difference in attitude, feelings of heaviness or lightness in your body, and clarity or confusion of thought. Develop your own personalized descriptive language to articulate any fluctuations you observe. The overall questions to reflect on are: "What is my energy level now?" and "How or why has it changed?" Be prepared to record notes on your energy level at least once an hour from morning to night.

Try This

MOTION AND EMOTION

After completing the Energy Monitor exercise, you may have noticed many obvious situations that affect your energy level throughout the day. This exercise is designed to help organize your observations in a way that captures the situations that increase or decrease your energy. Following are some sample situations and their perceived effect on an individual's energy level.

Emotional or Physical	Situation	Effect on Energy Level		
		Increase	Neutral	Decrease
Emotional	laughing out loud	X		
Emotional	arguing with a partner			X
Emotional	listening to a friend complain about work			X
Physical	standing in line for 20 minutes			X
Physical	watching two hours of TV		X	
Emotional	thinking about a disagreement with a boss			X
Emotional	worrying about paying the bills			X
Physical	exercising at the gym for 60 minutes	X		

Now, add your own real-life physical or emotional situations and note their effect on your energy level. If you feel a situation has no effect on your energy level, mark it as neutral.

Emotional or Physical	Situation	Effect on Energy Level		
		Increase	Neutral	Decrease

Total up the columns: Increase energy   _____

Decrease energy   _____

Neutral energy   _____

Synthesis Questions: Do you see a balance of energy in your activities and involvements? Which area reflects the highest decrease in energy? Which area brings you the most increase in energy? Can you see any patterns? How are you compensating or balancing your energy?

Try This

FINDING FOOD FOR ENERGY

See if you can step aside from the advertising about energy drinks, high and low carb sources, no fat, pure protein, and the endless lists of diet and nutritional do's and don'ts. If possible, temporarily adopt the belief that your body naturally knows what type and amount of food and drink is most healthy for it at all times. Also presume that whatever foods or liquids you need throughout the day are readily accessible to you, conveniently and freshly prepared. Now, go through your day and keep a written record of the *ideal* foods and drinks you would choose to keep your energy level balanced and your system running clean. Compare this record to the *actual* food and drink choices you made.

The important question to reflect on is what choices will you make to *change the quality* of your daily food and drink intake? You actually know what is good for you in most cases, but convenient access to prepackaged, processed foods makes eating fresh and clean a real challenge.

Make a commitment to change something about your food and drink intake and stick to it for at least one week. If you can change one habit for one week, move on to sustaining better choices for longer periods.

ASSETS AND CHALLENGES TO WELL-BEING

When you go to a physician, you are presented with an extensive questionnaire that asks you to account for any history of disease in your family, along with any current health concerns. Genetic heritage, cultural influences, the environment, and personal choices about what you do to and with your body and mind all affect your health. Your values, principles, and belief systems are the ultimate determiners of how you define your health and treat your ailments.

Health limitations can vary from reading glasses to terminal diseases. Some health problems can be prevented or deterred, while others occur by accident, genetics, or are precipitated by lifestyle choices. In this next exercise, you will make your own accounting of your top five health challenges and the ways in which you are enhancing your health.

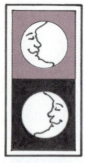

For Your Journal

Companion
Website

ACCOUNTING FOR HEALTH

*Please respond to the following in your journal or by using the **Journal Module** on the CW.*

Take a moment to list your top five health concerns—real or feared. Then, make note of five ways you can nurture your health on a consistent basis.

Concern	Nurture
Headaches	Reduce stress by taking a yoga class

COMMON SENSE AND UNCOMMON AWARENESS

If you have completed all of the self-assessments so far, you are probably becoming acutely aware of the variety of energy states you experience and how they might be directly related to how you manage your health. The assessments are designed to point toward the vast array of causes that degenerate and re-create your vitality on a daily basis. Generally, people do not have this type of awareness, and even though they may know that they are experiencing low energy at times, they may not have viewed it as a state that could create long-term patterns of illness and interfere with the ability to learn.

It is very important to recognize when and why you are experiencing low energy so that you don't get caught in a downward spiral. It is your personal responsibility to relentlessly call on methods to nurture and energize yourself until you are back in balance. If you learn to conserve your energy, then you will be more resilient in the face of difficulties.

Energy Conservation

When you expend your energy, you engage important *life resources*, including physical strength, time, emotion, attention, and clarity of mind. One alternative always at your disposal is intentionally conserving your vital energy by limiting your *unconscious expenditures of effort*. Here are some examples to think about:

- Stop all *unnecessary* tension. Do a body scan and intentionally relax each area of your body. Locate areas of tension in your shoulders, jaws, eyebrows, hands, legs—one by one, let the tensions go.
- Stop all *unnecessary* behaviors such as chewing gum, fiddling with pens, and talking.
- Stop all *unnecessary* thoughts. Use your mind only to work on problems and situations *in the present moment*. Do not think about the past or worry about the future.

If you can carry out any of these experiments in energy conservation over more than a few hours, you will likely notice a change in energy. The energy accumulated may actually feel somewhat uncomfortable. This type of energy is often called "nervous energy," and is usually viewed as something that must be used up quickly. Nervous energy can, however, be put to work for you if you learn how to redirect it.

Focusing Extra Energy

When you have to sit still, remain calm, focus, or rest, having too much energy can be challenging. Excessive mental energy can take the form of obsessive or troubled thoughts and cause sleepless nights and exhaustion. When you experience an overload of mental energy and can't stop thinking about something, a productive alternative to calm the mind and redirect the energy is to do something with a physical focus. It's the perfect time to exercise, wax the car, or clean the entire house.

A busy mind can seem to be an insurmountable distraction. Moving excess energy from the mental to the physical realm is more difficult when you are in a situation that requires you to be still and focus. In this situation, use your mental energy to visualize a focal point. Making a strong image in your mind's eye can help calm an overactive mind.

Refocusing or conserving extra physical energy is accomplished by shifting to mental energy when you engage your body. For example, taking a bike ride or long walk can be used as a time to memorize terminology, rehearse scenarios, or reflect on problem solving. It is the shifting from an entirely physical activity to splitting your efforts between mental and physical activities that brings a more dynamic result.

Conserving emotional energy begins with limiting the *expression* of negative emotions. This statement does not mean that you are to deny or suppress what you are feeling. Instead, what is suggested is that you offer minimal expression to negativity. The more you talk (internally or externally) about why you are upset, the more entangled you are likely to become in the negative emotional state. You may have heard the saying, "Stop complaining and DO something about it!" The idea is that you will have more energy and clarity to do something about whatever is upsetting you if you do not feed the negativity with your mind and words. Negative emotions that are not expressed or fed with thoughts tend to be short lived. Instead of leaving you with a feeling of prolonged drama and upset, you are freer to direct your energy into more pleasant and productive expressions.

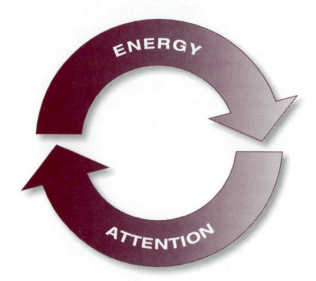

ENERGY AND ATTENTION

Chapter 3 explained that your energy follows your attention because your attention and energy levels are directly connected. When your energy is low, it is nearly impossible to keep your attention focused. Even when your energy is at its highest, it can be quickly exhausted by the demands of attention. It takes considerable effort to hold your attention on something for more than a few minutes. It is just like trying to hold a heavy weight in the air. Eventually, you just don't have anymore energy and your attention drops off. If you observe this process carefully in yourself, chances are that your mind will wander either to something that boosts your energy or something that drains your energy. When you begin to see how deeply energy and attention are interrelated, conserving and nurturing your energy becomes instrumental to your ability to successfully navigate life.

CULTIVATING NEUTRAL ENERGY

Neutral energy is cultivated by your awareness and intentional choices. Emotionally, you begin by managing the expression of negative emotions; you learn how to practice *detachment*. It is possible to be detached, yet stay completely involved. When you become emotionally "caught up," you limit your possible responses to a situation. For example, your friend leaves the door open and the dogs escape. If you get upset and angry, expending your energy by criticizing and blaming, then you have less energy to go catch the dogs. If you can detach from your emotional upset, you will realize that you will get more help catching the dogs simply by letting go of your need to blame. Detaching and attending to the matter at hand saves time and energy. It does not mean you don't care, it just means you are using detachment as a method of creating a peaceful and efficient resolution. Through detachment, you simply accept what is happening without blaming, and you can then make clearer, less emotionally colored decisions.

Mentally, neutral energy is cultivated by developing states of inner stillness. Meditation, prayer, and guided imagery are a few examples of how the noise from self-talk and the barrage of thoughts is tuned out. Even 10 minutes a day of "thinking about nothing" can help release your mind from the endless demands of your thoughts. Emptying your mind for brief intervals is like pressing the reset button.

Physically, you can work toward neutral energy by eating fresh, clean foods, exercising and taking in larger doses of oxygen, and avoiding toxins. You enhance your natural physical energies when you relax and unwind in healthy environments that feed your senses with comfort, beauty, and pleasure. Use awareness and intention to support adjustments to your lifestyle and move closer to being well and remaining calm and clear in the face of life's many challenges and difficulties.

Student Perspective

ENERGY AND HEALTH

After starting college, it did not take long to realize that my understanding and use of my personal energy was changing drastically. I never could have predicted that the new demands I placed on myself to maintain my academics and keep up with the rest of my life would be so difficult to handle. I always saw myself as a sort of a Superwoman, but my experiences in the college environment proved me wrong. When I first began attending classes, I felt like I could take on the world, and it showed in my choice of activities and courseload. I signed up for everything, accepted every extra credit assignment, jumped right into an

honors program and never thought twice about my choices. I didn't care if it took overnight cramming sessions, giving up all the parties and recreation time, and skipping meals—I was bound and determined to be a successful college student. I was fired up and ready to tackle anything thrown at me!

After just the first few months of school, I experienced a huge difference in the amount and type of energy I had. I quickly found myself struggling to get things done, stay awake, and feel alert. I realized that I spent a large part of my day experiencing anxiety and stress, something that was not a problem for me in the past. I started getting sick and always felt like something was "wrong." In only a short time, I found myself feeling tired, drained, unfocused, and even lethargic a great deal of the time. My lack of energy began to affect my performance in school—I was struggling to get started on assignments, taking naps instead of studying for exams, daydreaming during lectures, and making up excuses to stay home and get some rest instead of going to class. I kept telling myself that it was "just the way it is in college." Short of quitting school, I did not see any way to stop feeling so out of sorts and regain my normal sense of well-being.

When I finally forced myself to sit down and look at what I was experiencing, I realized that I was living in both extremes of the energy spectrum—I had not achieved balance. I started out with very high, undirected energy that soon brought me to a stage of burnout. Then, I hit a very low energy level and was unconsciously *making* myself tired, sick, and lethargic through the attitudes I held and the attention I gave to negative influences. My focus and health were failing because of the energy drains I created for myself, and until I got control of those, my attention and concentration could not improve.

These days, I still experience fluctuations in my energy levels, but I try to stay aware and take the steps necessary to bring myself back to center when I feel I am getting out of balance. It is not always easy, but sometimes, all it takes is realizing how I am feeling to help me alleviate and move past the things that adversely affect me. If I am feeling anxious, stressed, or antsy, I try to do something to relieve the extra energy. If I am experiencing a low energy level, I don't try to push myself because I understand now that I must replenish my energy before trying to concentrate and get my work done. I learned to remain self-aware and put my own well-being before my assignments and responsibilities because I know I can't do my best work if my energy level is at either extreme.

REFLECTION QUESTIONS

1. What are the indicators that signal you to take action and rebalance?
2. How do you replenish your energy when you are feeling burned out?

SUMMARY

This chapter looked at **energy** as the basis of physical well-being and mental clarity. The self-assessments created an awareness of the different energy states you experience, what types of situations create fluctuations in your energy, and the methods with which you manage your well being.

Your energy follows your attention. Your attention and energy levels are directly connected. When your energy is low, it is nearly impossible to keep your attention focused. Internalized **energy drains** include indecision, confusion, negative emotions, and repetitious thoughts. To balance these types of depleting processes, it is important to keep a repertoire of calming, relaxing, and reenergizing methods and activities accessible to your daily routine. One way to **gather energy** is by invigorating your body and mind through movements and open postures that generate more oxygen to your system and decrease tension. Yoga, working out, or even a good brisk walk can help you gather good energy. **Conserve energy** by limiting unnecessary talking and eliminating unnecessary tension in your face, limbs, or shoulders.

Neutral energy is cultivated by managing the expression of negative emotions, and by releasing your mind from the endless barrage of thoughts.

Genetic heritage, cultural influences, the environment, and personal choices about what you do to and with your body and mind affects your health. Your values, principles, and belief systems are the ultimate determiners of how you define your health and create well being.

Case Studies

CASE STUDY 4.1

Toxic Workplace—Energy

Franklin is an intelligent and outgoing young man. He was very excited when offered a job at the local office complex doing bookkeeping work for an accounting firm. The pay was great, the hours and benefits were outstanding—it was a dream come true.

Six months have passed, and Franklin is not as happy as he was when he began working at the firm. He gets migraine headaches, feels tired a good deal of the time, and has had the flu three times since his employment began. Because there have not been any other changes to his lifestyle, he believes that the symptoms he is currently experiencing may be linked to the workplace.

The following is a brief list of physical, tangible problems that Franklin feels might be affecting him at his office:

- ventilation system
- lighting
- paint
- décor and plants
- water source
- machinery and equipment
- germs

There are other things that Franklin also considers relevant:

- stress of his job
- treatment by coworkers
- treatment by superiors
- long hours and overtime

REFLECTION QUESTIONS

1. What steps can Franklin take to uncover and deal with the source of his problems? Choose a few of the possible attributors and comment on how he might deal with them without giving up the job.
2. Discuss in groups the various ways that things that are not obviously toxic can affect people. Relate personal experiences if applicable, and focus on the various ways these toxic influences can be overcome.

CASE STUDY 4.2

Energy and Attention

Paula has difficulty staying focused when she is reading or working on her writing project. One thing she noticed is that she has many distractions and is constantly getting up to tend to things when she is trying to study or write. She worries about her ability to make a good grade on the paper. At times, she is so restless that she has to jump up from the computer and walk aimlessly around the house. As she goes from room to room, she finds little things that must be done—she hangs up a jacket, feeds the fish, and wipes down the countertop. She sits for a minute and begins to type. Then, the dog comes in and distracts her attention. She goes to let the dog outside and sees that a potted plant has blown over, so she cleans up the broken pieces. When she sits down to work again, she feels tired and remembers she has to make the bed. During the next two hours, Paula expends all of the energy she needs to focus on writing. She begins to feel frustrated—she cannot focus on or think of the right words to capture the ideas for her paper. The more frustrated she gets, the more she feels her energy dropping.

REFLECTION QUESTIONS

1. What can Paula do to reenergize?
2. What simple things could Paula have done to *conserve* her energy so she could stay focused on the paper?
3. Are Paula's external distractions the only source of her energy loss?
4. What is one of the best ways for Paula to approach her project with renewed energy and attention?

Demonstration of Competency

*Please respond to the following in your journal or by using the **Demonstration of Competency Module** on the CW.*

Imagine waking up each morning feeling refreshed and energized. All day, you have a focused, calm, clear mind and a strong, relaxed, vital body. Write a short essay that explains how you might create or maintain this state for yourself. Include a detailed accounting of any bad habits or negative attitudes that you will replace with energizers.

Additional references and resources for chapter topics can be found at **www.prenhall.com/gray**.

Emotional Intelligence

SELF-MASTERY

Education is the ability to listen to almost anything without losing your temper or your self-confidence.

—ROBERT FROST (1874–1963)

L earners who excel in higher education use the emotional intelligence qualities of self-awareness and self-regulation to avoid procrastination, act with integrity, and focus their attention on creating optimal learning experiences. Emotionally intelligent students are self-motivated and take responsibility for their choices.

The qualities of emotional intelligence have received important emphasis in corporate settings over the last decade. Studies show that the most highly valued employees have mastered such aspects of emotional intelligence as self-motivation, integrity, and social competence. It is a person's ability to interact amicably, communicate clearly, and assess accurately that makes him or her an outstanding employee. These inner qualities can actually matter more than academic training when determining promotions and pay increases.

This chapter examines the aspects of emotional intelligence and how it can impact your success in both the classroom and the workplace.

What If . . .

What if your grades were based on your attitude toward learning? What grade would you give your attitude?

WHAT IS EMOTIONAL INTELLIGENCE?

Emotional intelligence (EI) is measured by your *attitude* toward others and yourself. Emotional intelligence is exemplified by optimism, or staying positive, in the face of obstacles and failures. It is also an attitude of gratitude, where one see opportunities instead of limitations when the going gets tough. In the mid-1990s, author Daniel Goleman wrote several books that popularized the concept of emotional intelligence. Goleman claimed that EI is actually a better indicator of success in life and the workplace than IQ. Some of the qualities of EI that Goleman feels are most important include self-awareness, self-responsibility, and social competence.

A positive or negative outlook dramatically affects how your world and the people in it respond to you. When you are in a negative inner state, you can actually amplify misfortunes and unintentionally draw more difficulties and anxiety into your path. Does this scenario sound familiar? You wake up late and are in a rush to get to work. As you hurry to fix breakfast, you spill coffee on your shirt, which further delays you and inflames your irritability. While trying to get out the door, you bang your elbow. Now, in pain and irritated, you fumble with your keys getting in the car and drop your book bag, spilling everything out on the street.

As you know from your own experiences, sometimes these scenarios even get worse—speeding tickets, accidents, further emotional upsets and drama with people you encounter, and all variety of mishaps. If you reflect on it, you'll recall examples of how your inner state created or intensified negative external situations (see Figure 5.1). The question remains: *If you really believe that changing your inner emotional state can make life easier, then why don't you do it?* Why suffer or continue to have upsetting things occur?

In theory, emotionally intelligent people *can change* their inner state by taking charge of themselves and their emotions. Emotional intelligence is synonymous with managing emotional states (see Figure 5.2). Emotions are transitory, meaning that they change and change often. People prolong emotional states by *thinking* about how they feel—thus, the saying, "I just can't stop thinking about what happened." If they stop thinking about how they feel and do not fuel their emotions with *thoughts*, either reliving upsetting experiences or worrying about things that might happen in the future, then, the emotion will simply pass.

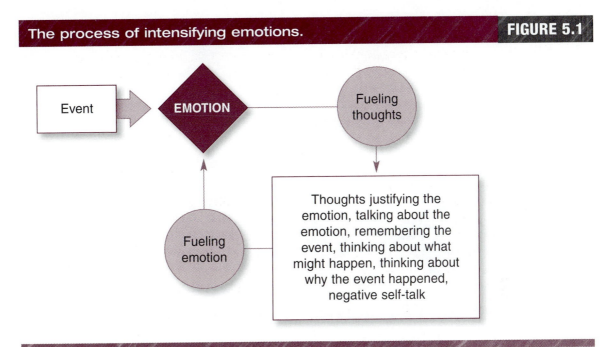

The process of intensifying emotions.   **FIGURE 5.1**

The transitory nature of emotions is especially easy to observe in children who can be coaxed to stop a crying fit. Their emotions can move from crying to laughter in a matter of minutes. It is not until you use language and either talk or think about your emotions that they become enlarged and create feelings that take charge of you. For example, if you are nervous about a job interview, you may have *inner self-talk* that confirms your fears. You may think, "I probably don't have the type of job experience they are looking for." Or "What if I can't answer the questions they ask?" Externally, you are expressing your nervousness by telling your friends about how petrified you are about going on the interview or that you are afraid they will want more references than you have. Talking about your fears and thinking about them can intensify the emotional state. Not focusing on the emotions reduces their intensity.

It is in the balancing of thinking and feeling that emotional intelligence is applied. The idea is to use the heart to change the mind or the mind to change the heart. For example, when you find yourself in an irritated state, no matter how justified, you can manage that state so it does not interfere with how professionally you behave. *Observing* your emotional state and then making a conscious *choice* about the type of response you want to express is an aspect of emotional intelligence that requires self-awareness.

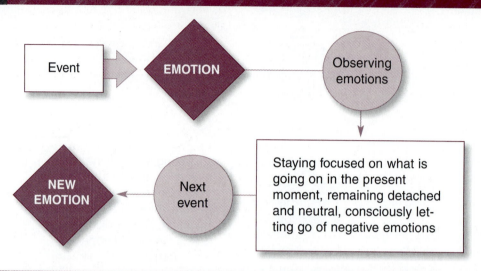

FIGURE 5.2   Balancing emotions.

Try This

To have a very basic experience practicing self-awareness, ask yourself the following questions right now:

- What am I thinking about?
- What is my overall emotional state?
- What do I see, hear, and sense with my body both inwardly and outwardly?

 Take about 10–15 minutes to *observe without judgment* and write the answers to these questions in as much detail as you possibly can. If you find you do not know the answers or are only vaguely aware of them, then write about what might be stopping you from feeling or thinking clearly.

SELF-AWARENESS

Self-awareness can be defined as observing your thoughts, sensations, and emotions without judgment. It is the experience of witnessing yourself from a neutral perspective. Self-awareness is not self-consciousness. Generally, self-consciousness means an uncomfortable state of awareness where you are concerned about how you think others perceive you. For example, you may be self-conscious about speaking in front of a group, fearing you will get tongue-tied. Self-awareness, on the other hand, is a process of simply *noticing* your discomfort with the situation and accounting for your fears and emotions to yourself without the negative self-talk. Awareness is not the same as thinking or analyzing. Awareness is just seeing, hearing, observing, and acknowledging. Awareness does not try to blame, accuse, or correct. Self-awareness is *watching your experience* of how you feel or think.

If you become intensely self-aware, you might face uncomfortable emotions or physical conditions that you otherwise disassociate from. Self-awareness can be painfully revealing, but this is often the first step or incentive to make important life-changing efforts. This is why it is essential to refrain from being critical or hard on yourself when you are just observing your state. Self-awareness is a barometer that informs you of when you should make renewed efforts to move into closer alignment with your goals, values, and principles—it should not be used to beat yourself up for perceived shortcomings or failures. The key is to let the observations simply show you where you are in your process.

Honest self-assessment is a tool for positive change and motivated learning. When you are self-critical, you drain yourself of energy that is otherwise needed to make efforts to change. You also run the risk of creating a self-fulfilling prophecy. For example, when you tell yourself that you won't be able to finish a project by a deadline, you are affirming that possibility and giving it more power by *thinking it might be true*. Negative self-talk keeps you stuck in self-defeating behaviors. Acknowledging your strengths and weaknesses without judgment is a key sign of emotional intelligence.

For star performance in all jobs in every field, emotional competence is twice as important as purely cognitive abilities.

—DANIEL GOLEMAN

Student Perspective

SELF-CONFIDENCE

Tell me if this sounds familiar to you. You open up the current course catalog and start reading over the classes offered for the coming semester. The mental dialog begins, "Calculus? Nope, I am not good with numbers. Physics? Nope, I am not really a good science student. American history? Nope, I never could remember dates. Film analysis? Nope, I never did well analyzing other people's work. Drawing? No way, I could never even draw stick figures." You reach the end of the catalog and proclaim, "They just aren't offering anything good this term."

It is one thing to be genuinely disinterested in something—this is a perfectly valid reasoning skill. It is something else entirely to pass up opportunities for learning and growth because of some internal belief that you won't be successful. Not signing up for that calculus course (even though you are interested in it) just because you "aren't good at math" is a self-defeating and, ultimately, destructive choice. It is self-defeating because you are limiting yourself and therefore, limiting your potential to learn new things. If you only take classes that you know you are "good at," what are you actually going to learn? This is eventually a self-destructive behavior because if you really are not good at something, the only way to become better at it is to engage it and try. If you are not willing to try, you will not get any better. If you won't take a science class right now because you are a weak science student, you will stay a weak science student. If you really want to get anything out of the college experience, you must be confident in your ability to learn and allow your internal motivation to guide you—even if what it guides you toward might be a little intimidating. If you are interested in something, take the risk and try it out! You may find that your negative self-talk was wrong—you are better at some things than you give yourself credit for.

REFLECTION QUESTIONS

What types of classes do you avoid and why? If you experience fears or apprehensions, what causes you to feel that way about your abilities? Are your ideas about your abilities really valid, or might they be unwarranted? Explain your experiences.

ATTITUDES AND AWARENESS

There is a direct relationship between self-awareness and self-confidence. As you begin to focus more on being aware of your thoughts, feelings, and sensations, the depth of your life experience increases. As experience becomes more impressive and full, you actually learn more, not only about yourself, but also about life and living. This quality of life experience gives you a firm foundation for better critical thinking. Your critical-thinking skills are based in your life experiences. The more aware you are of the many aspects, emotions, and sensations of your life, the more memorable and clear your references and reflections on those experiences will be.

Because not all experiences are pleasant or comforting, your inner self-talk becomes the guiding force in determining whether you process your experiences as self-empowering or self-defeating. By this point in your life, you have *learned* attitudes that act as filters on your experiences. You have likes and dislikes and fixed opinions about many perspectives. Once you see that your attitudes alone seriously affect your ability to learn and live well, you would think you could simply change them at will. Yet, attitudes are even more challenging to alter than some substance addictions. You are more attached than you realize to your views and opinions about yourself and the world, even if holding on to those views actually makes you more miserable.

A willingness to stay positive, grateful, and optimistic in the face of difficult or unpleasant circumstances is not easy—it requires a firm commitment to improving the quality of your life and experiences. When you notice that your attitude is in a negative state, it is important to acknowledge that emotional state, examine the situation, and make a conscious effort to change the way you see things. This type of self-regulation makes the difference between travesty and victory.

Student Perspective

SELF-ESTEEM

The transition into college, for me, was absolutely paralyzing. I experienced an enormous amount of anxiety, stress, and fear during my first few months of school. A fear of failure, feelings of inadequacy, the stresses of time management, and a strong notion of "not fitting in" plagued me. I realized early on that as a student—not just academically but of life itself—I had to become capable of overcoming my fears and anxieties or I could not succeed. This was absolutely terrifying for me! All of a sudden, I was forced to learn to understand myself, relate to those around me, accept responsibility for my actions, and share myself with the world. In the process, I was forced to assess and examine myself at a level that was quite uncomfortable for me and come face to face with things inside of me that were really unpleasant.

I found myself making excuses for sitting at the back of the class, avoiding study groups, and not answering questions in class. In my first month of school, I never ventured beyond the classrooms that my courses were held in. I did not eat lunch or even take coffee breaks on campus. I avoided other students and did not even consider joining campus activities or organizations. I became completely invisible. I told myself that I was just not a social person and that I did not have to fit in, make friends, or be recognized. I just wanted to go to class, learn the material, and get my degree. The most troubling realization for me was accepting the fact that I was only fooling myself—I was really afraid. Because of that fear, I was allowing myself to miss out on a great many positive experiences and opportunities for learning.

That simple act of noticing and accepting my own fears and anxieties has made all the difference in my education. Once I accepted my feelings, I was able to overcome them. I gradually started to participate more in class and found that what I had to say was welcomed and respected by those in the class. I started sitting closer to the front of the classroom and discovered that I actually learned more and maintained my attention better. I started interacting with my classmates outside the classroom and discovered that I was making some wonderful friends. I joined and became active in social groups and campus activities and discovered that I had a great deal to offer the college community. It was not easy or entirely comfortable, but learning to face my feelings and work with them has really helped me to succeed.

REFLECTION QUESTIONS

Write about how your self-confidence affects your attitude about your studies. Do you have concerns about your study skills or the transition to college life that have affected your self-esteem?

SELF-RESPONSIBILITY

This aspect of emotional intelligence includes the roots of self-mastery. Self-responsibility means showing restraint, delaying gratification, and exercising self-control. It is also known as self-regulation, which refers to how you manage your desires and bolster your motivation. Students and employees who take initiative, find solutions, and follow through on their promises are exemplifying self-responsibility. This trait of emotional intelligence also accounts for the ability to accept responsibility for how you respond to what life brings instead of placing blame on others.

DELAYING GRATIFICATION

In today's American culture, the idea of patiently and calmly waiting for anything may seem alien. Most businesses sell their products or ideas based on instant credit, immediate pleasure, and easy access. We expect to press a button, swipe a credit card, or click a mouse and receive responses and products quicker than we can think. Waiting for anything is an inconvenience and a source of frustration. Yet, the old adage that "patience is a virtue" still rings true as a guiding principle in research studies of successful students and employees. Studies continually show that the majority of children who exert self-discipline at a young age grow to be adults with jobs that require high integrity and consistent follow through. The idea that good things come to those who wait may be a secret formula for surviving the disappointments of modern "conveniences." So far, we have not escaped waiting in traffic or waiting in line at a bank or store. Even waiting for a fax or an e-mail may seem to take too much time.

Delaying gratification means being able to make good use of our time when we do have to wait. Whether waiting for a stoplight or waiting for a better job opportunity, it is how we utilize the space in between that gives it value. Being irritated, frustrated, and angry at waiting might seem a justifiable response; however, those negative emotions have a price. Fueling or harboring unpleasant feelings further exhausts us.

Self-control refers to the act of mastering the appropriate display of emotions in the presence of others. It means limiting the expression of negative emotions. For example, we may have every reason to be outraged when a salesperson ignores us and helps someone else; however, we must carefully choose our response. If we stay upset and keep thinking about it all day, it can make us respond in anger to another unconnected life situation and inadvertently create another negative interaction with someone else. On the other hand, if we creatively use the waiting time while the clerk assists someone else to relax our body, practice breathing meditation, or recall the terminology we are trying to memorize, time not only passes faster, but we have reenergized our self.

Waiting also give us opportunities for creative visualization. We can practice bringing ourselves closer to our goals by mentally imagining the details. It is also an opportunity for planning or problem solving. Delaying gratification means living creatively in the present moment and not squandering time by expending ourselves on draining emotions or activities that detract from our goals.

Student Perspective

SELF-RESPONSIBILITY AND PRIORITIZING

OK, so we all understand that college is a place of learning. We are here to expand our minds and enrich our intellect—and meet girls/guys, make friends, have fun. Yes, college is the place to do it all—as long as "doing it all" doesn't conflict with what we truly wish to accomplish. The truth is "all work and no play" can be very frustrating and we should have some fun once in a while. It is a good thing to try to seek a balance between the serious, stressful, and demanding aspects of college and the fun, wild, and exciting ones. The key word here is balance, and balance requires self-awareness and responsible decision making.

You will undoubtedly come across the "Friday night problem" at least once during your academic career. If you haven't figured it out yet, the Friday night problem is the hated decision of choosing between the party and the paper you have to write; the nightclub and the nine pages of math problems due Monday; the bonfire or the biology homework. And it isn't just a Friday problem; this one can pop up any day at any time—a choice between the new episode of your favorite TV show and the extra half hour of studying; the lunch date with that great new somebody or the study group; the trip to the beach or the boring statistics lecture. The real question isn't WHAT you are going to do; it is WHY you are going to do it.

Examining your needs and being aware of the choice at hand is a great first step. Only you really know for certain if you have the time to attend a party or if that work really must get done now. Only you can recognize when you really have to take a break from the workload and when you really should get cracking on the books. Only you can figure out which of the choices is the right one because only you can identify your own needs, values, and goals. Only you can judge what action you should take in order to achieve them. Ask yourself WHY before you make your decision. Consider the benefits of each option, keeping your values and goals in mind. Identify outside influences and be honest with yourself about your reasons. You will find that all of your choices become more appropriate and beneficial when you exercise self-responsibility and awareness.

REFLECTION QUESTIONS

When making decisions about work and play, what type of things do you consider? Are your choices usually beneficial to your goals? Explain this using an example of a choice you made.

Try This

BALANCING EXTREMES

The ability to take constructive criticism or feedback without becoming defensive or overreacting is a characteristic of emotional intelligence. It can be a challenge to remain detached when someone you love or care about sees you in an unfavorable light and offers unsolicited ideas about how you might improve. It is not easy to have a teacher or supervisor tell you that you have performed in a substandard manner. One way you might respond is to become defensive, blaming the poor judgment or inadequacies of the other person. You may offer up excuses or reasons that circumstances worked against you. You could choose to work obsessively to correct the area of criticism. In your fearful zeal to improve, you sometimes sacrifice your well-being or sanity.

In this exercise, describe how you react to criticism. Provide an example of a time when you were criticized or corrected. How did you respond? How might you have responded if you were totally self-responsible?

SOCIAL COMPETENCE

The key words that capture the essence of social competence are *adaptability* and *empathy*. These emotional intelligence skills determine how we handle all types of relationships.

We use empathy as a connector to others when we are sincere listeners. Many times, we solve our own problems just by speaking about them to an empathic listener. The ability to inquire of others and lend an ear is a social skill that creates positive exchanges. People tend to enjoy talking about themselves, and a good listener is usually noticed and appreciated. Listening deeply is a powerful healing tool that we can cultivate with our loved ones as well as total strangers.

Today, we find ourselves working and living in increasingly culturally diverse environments that require us to respect and relate well to people from a variety of backgrounds. Being sensitive and aware of cultural differences involves being empathetic. Although we cannot completely understand all of the nuances of cultures that we have not been immersed in, we can understand others through the universality of emotions. In this way, empathy connects us to different people. We develop tolerance and unbiased attitudes by sharing in the purity of the common language of emotions.

Student Perspective

MULTIPLE PERSPECTIVES

If you have been in the college environment for even a week, you have noticed that you are surrounded by a whole new set of people. You are going to find yourself in classes with people from every state in America and from many different countries. You may have professors who come from unfamiliar areas of the world. Your classmates may hail from diverse ethnicities, political backgrounds, and religions. They may speak different languages or hold different levels of understanding as to the usage of English. This can be a real culture shock, especially if your contact with diversity has been limited.

You are in a wonderful position to begin learning and adjusting to the diversity of your world! You are also in a position where it is easy to put your foot in your mouth and unwittingly offend, embarrass, or cause dis-

comfort to the people around you if you do not make an effort to respect the cultural differences of your new community. Imagine a total stranger who, upon meeting you for the first time, comes very close to you while speaking and reaches out to hug you! You don't even know him, and he wants a hug! In our culture, this is not considered normal behavior, but in some parts of the Middle East, it is customary and a sign of respect to embrace when you meet someone. There are places in the world where shaking hands is not practiced, so a person from such a culture might be offended or frightened if you extended your hand as is customary here.

By remaining mindful of diversity and making a conscious effort to be aware of the differences between cultures, you can avoid hurting or offending someone. You don't have to agree with the beliefs or practices of others, but some sensitivity and open-mindedness sure goes a long way. More importantly, by remaining open-minded and learning more about the diverse cultures around you, you have the opportunity to become a more understanding, adaptable, humanistic, and tolerant human being.

REFLECTION QUESTIONS

Describe your level of exposure to different world cultures. Do you consider yourself adaptable and open-minded toward diversity or is it uncomfortable for you? Discuss some of your own experiences with diversity issues.

ADAPTABILITY

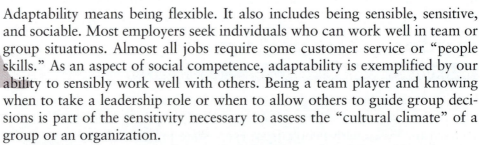

Adaptability means being flexible. It also includes being sensible, sensitive, and sociable. Most employers seek individuals who can work well in team or group situations. Almost all jobs require some customer service or "people skills." As an aspect of social competence, adaptability is exemplified by our ability to sensibly work well with others. Being a team player and knowing when to take a leadership role or when to allow others to guide group decisions is part of the sensitivity necessary to assess the "cultural climate" of a group or an organization.

Unspoken expectations for certain behaviors and social considerations are present in almost any group setting, especially in corporate offices. For example, many companies still have dress codes or expectations for the appearance of their employees. Other companies are more relaxed and allow casual attire. The emotionally intelligent person either asks directly or makes careful note of what seems to be the trend and works toward a reasonable balance.

Adaptability is also related to the ability to blend in or stand out in group situations. More importantly, a finely tuned self-awareness should provide clues as to whether someone is standing out too much—meaning he or she is almost unapproachable—or standing out too little and seems invisible. Sometimes, in an effort to broadcast our uniqueness and independence, we inadvertently make ourselves unapproachable. On the other hand, if we blend in too much and keep a very low profile in group settings, we feel left out or ignored when no one seems to notice us. Being adaptable allows us to arrange for a balance in our presence and demeanor that is appropriate for creating interaction and relationship in groups.

For Your Journal

DISCOVERING IMPLICIT EXPECTATIONS

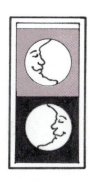

*Please respond to the following in your journal or by using the **Journal Module** on the CW.*

Implicit expectations are unspoken ideas about what you really want or need. A job description usually lists skills or educational requirements. In addition to those measurable and verifiable criteria, most seasoned employment interviewers are also looking for internal qualities such as reliability and trustworthiness—generally, someone of outstanding character. These are their implicit expectations of a "good" employee (in addition to training and education).

To discover some of your implicit expectations, list what you think are the top five qualities of a good teacher in the left column of the following chart. These are implicit expectations because most students already know, just like you do, what makes up the qualities of a good teacher. Next, rate yourself on the same criteria from the teachers' perspective in the right column. As a student, which qualities do you already know you might improve on?

QUALITIES OF A GOOD TEACHER	HOW I RATE MYSELF ON EACH QUALITY
	1 = I am a star. 2 = I could do better. 3 = I need major improvement.
1	
2	
3	
4	
5	

You can use this same chart to list the top five qualities of a good politician or the top five qualities of a good life partner. This exercise shows that we have many implicit or unspoken expectations about what characteristics are suitable for various life roles. Being able to adapt to the implicit expectations of your social interactions is a sign of emotional intelligence.

RESPONDING TO NEGATIVE RELATIONSHIPS AND CONFLICTS

Emotional intelligence also helps us position ourselves to respond positively even in the face of negative or antagonistic relationships. Self-awareness alerts us with red flags when we are involved in an interaction that is draining our energy or affecting our emotional health. Unfortunately, not all negative relationships are avoidable. We have to work with people who may irritate us, and we have to live with family or friends who we may not see eye to eye with. The stress, upset, and heartbreak that occurs when we are in the grip of a distressing interaction with someone dramatically impacts our health, robs us of energy, and destroys our focus.

Ultimately, emotional intelligence is about managing our emotions. When confronted with draining and unhealthy relationships, there is one basic principle to remember: *Focus on changing yourself and not the other person.* In some situations, this may mean disengaging from contact or avoiding an antagonistic relationship. Other circumstances may require learning new communication techniques or making stronger attempts at problem resolution. Regardless of the means employed, using emotional intelligence requires that we take 100 percent responsibility for the outcomes of all of our relationships.

Student Perspective

ADAPTABILITY

Professors are intelligent, capable, and admirable in the eyes of the average college student. We look to them for guidance, understanding, information, and expertise, and we set some pretty high expectations. So, what happens when we discover that this icon of education, the professor, is just a human being like everyone else? Even worse, what if this human being is not someone we find particularly likable?

If your professor is arrogant or has other qualities you view as negative, there is nothing you can do about that. You are empowered, however, to do something about your attitude toward the situation. If you spend the class period thinking about how much you hate this person, you aren't learning. If you shudder at the thought of walking in the room, you are not creating a receptive learning state. If you walk out at the end of class and sit with your classmates complaining, not only are you wasting your time, but also the time of everyone else. Where is the sense in that? Are you actually going to jeopardize your academic performance because you don't like the professor? Exercising your self-awareness and control in this situation keeps you from allowing it to become a bad experience. You don't have to like the teacher—but you do have to show respect, uphold your responsibilities, learn the material, and succeed in the course. Maintain focus on these important aspects of the matter and accept responsibility for your role in achieving what you want from the course.

REFLECTION QUESTIONS

Have you ever encountered a professor whom you absolutely could not stand? What happened? How did you deal with the situation?

For Your Journal

MAKING SENSE OF NEW CONCEPTS

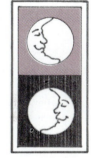

Please respond to the following in your journal or by using the **Journal Module** *on the CW.*

Define these concepts in *terms of your own experience.*

SELF-AWARENESS

_____

_____

_____

SELF-MOTIVATION

_____

_____

_____

SELF-RESPONSIBLE

_____

_____

_____

INTEGRITY

_____

_____

_____

EMPATHY

_____

_____

_____

POSITIVE ATTITUDES

_____

_____

_____

DELAYING GRATIFICATION

_____

_____

_____

ADAPTABILITY

_____

_____

_____

SUMMARY

This chapter focused on **emotional intelligence,** which involves intentional awareness, acceptance, and the use of your emotions for productive and beneficial means. Balancing emotions and thoughts, remaining optimistic, and experiencing gratitude are some of the key characteristics of an emotionally intelligent person. Emotional intelligence can actually be more important to overall success than standard intellect.

Self-awareness is the ability to observe yourself without judgment. By reflecting on your own feelings and thoughts, self-awareness helps guide you in making good choices. **Self-responsibility** is a willingness to accept that you are in control of your thoughts, behaviors, and actions without placing blame. It means showing restraint, delaying gratification, and exercising self-control. It is also known as self-regulation, which refers to how you manage your desires and bolster your motivation. **Delaying gratification** means living creatively in the present moment instead of pining toward a future event. It also refers to the ability to be patient and steadfast. Exercising self-responsibility and **self-motivation** empowers you to achieve your goals and increase the level of fulfillment in your life.

Emotional intelligence becomes most powerful in social interactions. Empathy, adaptability, and approachability are criteria for being socially competent. **Empathy** refers to your ability to understand others through the universality of emotions. **Adaptability** means being flexible. **Approachability** is connected to your ability to maintain an openness in your interactions with others.

Case Studies

CASE STUDY 5.1

Emotional Intelligence and Empathy

Paula has worked as an administrative assistant to the vice president of a mid-sized company for the past three years. She is indispensable to her boss because her attention to detail and proactive planning keeps the company a step ahead of the competition at every turn. She was named employee of the year and was awarded bonuses each Christmas for outstanding service to the company. Six months ago, the vice president retired and was replaced by Ms. Mazing. Paula has made every effort to be accommodating and supportive of Ms. Mazing's administrative style; however, during the past 30 days there were several occasions where Ms. Mazing openly criticized her in front of coworkers. For the first time during her employment, Paula was passed over for a bonus.

Because the tension during the last two days was unbearable, Paula decided to take things into her own hands and requested a private meeting with Ms. Mazing. Paula's mounting negative emotional state is fueling her thoughts prior to the meeting. She decided that she is willing to resign if Ms. Mazing does not give her the bonus. She also resolved to tell Ms. Mazing that she will not tolerate being publicly criticized. An hour before the meeting Ms. Mazing leaves Paula a voice-mail message postponing the meeting until next month because something more urgent came up. Paula is incensed and feels Ms. Mazing is completely ignoring her. After stewing about this turn of events for two days, Paula is prepared to barge into Ms. Mazing's office and refuse to leave until her complaints are heard. Minutes before her boss comes in to work, Paula takes a message from the pediatrician of Ms. Mazing's daughter. The message was: "Please call me immediately regarding your daughter's test results because the surgery must be scheduled within the next 48 hours." Moments later, Ms. Mazing steps through the office door and her eyes meet Paula's.

REFLECTION QUESTIONS

1. What should Paula do now that she knows Ms. Mazing's daughter is seriously ill? Should she allow that to have an effect on when she meets with Ms. Mazing and what she says to her? Why or why not?
2. If Paula acts emotionally intelligent, what feelings might she express in her next interaction with Ms. Mazing?
3. What might be Paula's thoughts before meeting with Ms. Mazing if she truly wishes to be a "supportive and accommodating" assistant?
4. How could Paula present her concerns to Ms. Mazing in an emotionally intelligent manner?
5. In the current situation, is there anything else Paula can do to act in a self-responsible manner?

CASE STUDY 5.2

Emotional Intelligence and Delayed Gratification

RJ has a habit that's killing him. No, it's not smoking, drinking, or drugging. RJ has a habit of killing time. He knows there are productive, important things he could be doing, but he has developed a slight addiction to screens. On average, RJ spends 50 hours a week looking at a screen. For example, each weekday evening, he plays Krikee—an interactive Internet game—for a total of 20 hours weekly. Then, on the weekends, he watches the sports channels for about seven hours and usually rents a couple of movies with his girlfriend on Friday night (three hours). While he's at work during the day, he surfs the Internet or plays games on his laptop in between customers, for another 20 hours a week.

RJ wants to get a better paying job. His girlfriend has urged him to get trained in multimedia design or computer programming so he can pursue his pastimes in a more productive manner. Although this idea does seriously interest RJ, he just can't see where he could make the time to add 30 hours a week of training into his current schedule. He doesn't consider himself a slacker, but he is closing in on the regional championships in Krikee, which has taken over three years to accomplish, and there are the NFL play-offs starting in two weeks.

RJ has spent 50 hours a week looking at screens for the past four years. Unless something changes, he will spend the next four years in the same manner. This adds up to almost 2.5 years of looking at a screen in an eight-year time frame.

REFLECTION QUESTIONS

1. How can RJ use emotional intelligence to stop killing time?
2. Explain how RJ might use self-awareness to change a habit.
3. Describe how and why delaying gratification might work for RJ.

CASE STUDY 5.3

Emotional Intelligence Self-Assessments

If you search for Emotional Intelligence on the Web, you will find several on-line emotional intelligence tests. These tests are designed to help the user assess his or her level of emotional intelligence and they offer suggestions and ideas to improve these aptitudes.

Refer to the links on the companion website or do your own on-line search and find one of these free assessment tests. After taking the test, reflect on the questions it asked and the responses you entered. Do you feel the assessment was helpful? What did you learn from the exercise? Do you feel that these types of assessments can accurately measure emotional intelligence? Why or why not? Would you suggest the use of assessment tools such as these to others?

Demonstration of Competency

Companion
Website

*Please respond to the following in your journal or by using the **Demonstration of Competency Module** on the* CW.

Rate your competency for the concepts listed below using this scale:

1 = no experiences or ideas   2 = a few ideas but no experience   3 = some experience
4 = I know all I need to know about this   5 = I am an expert

CONCEPT	RATING
Self-awareness	
Honest self-assessment	
Responding to criticism	
Empathic listening	
Trustworthiness	

Set a personal learning objective for any concept that you rated 1 or 2. Write a sentence stating what you will commit to do and how you plan to learn more about the concept during the next week.

_____

_____

_____

Additional references and resources for chapter topics can be found at **www.prenhall.com/gray**

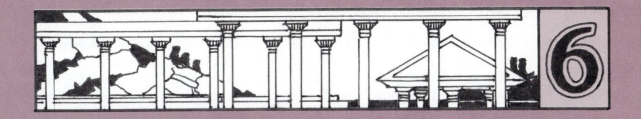

Integrity

MOTIVATION AND ACCOUNTABILITY

T he objective of this chapter is to help you develop and affirm the means and intentions to act from a position of integrity in life and learning. By aligning your intentions with your values and goals you become accountable to yourself first and then to others. Keeping your word and taking initiative are the beginnings of personal integrity.

What If . . .

What if people always kept their word? How would the world be different? Is it reasonable to expect people to keep the promises they make? What are some situations you can think of that might make breaking a promise acceptable?

DEFINING INTEGRITY

Politicians mislead us, CEOs cook the books, and we waste hundreds of hours getting questionable repairs done to shabby products and tolerating inferior services. In this day and age, it seems that integrity is not a popular trend and no longer a cultivated aspect of most peoples' character. Integrity is a rare and revered quality. Employers rejoice when they hire employees who consistently act with integrity. Consumers spread the word quickly about products that are built with integrity and services that are given in this manner. Integrity is a key feature of respected leaders.

So, what exactly makes actions and behaviors resound with integrity? Acts of integrity are purposeful and intentional actions that are based solidly in ethics, principles, or values. People acting with integrity are motivated to take initiative and are also accountable and trustworthy. In a culture where integrity seems to be on the decline, our individual responsibility to model and exemplify integrity becomes imperative.

I am sure that in estimating every man's value either in private or public life, a pure integrity is the quality we take first into calculation, and that learning and talents are only the second.

—THOMAS JEFFERSON (1743–1826)

SELF-MOTIVATION

Traditional educational systems teach that a test score or grade can measure intelligence. In many cases, students learn to master the educational system by memorizing information instead of learning how to learn. Some students who are motivated solely by grades or scores find out only what they have to know to get a specific grade and then do no more to get through their classes. This type of motivation is called *extrinsic,* meaning that some external source, such as grades or money, is the sole source of motivation.

In contrast, self-motivated learners generate a positive learning experience when they obtain an inner goal. For example, internal values or principles, such as trustworthiness or a passion for life, drive *intrinsically* motivated students or employees. Their sense of accomplishment may come from simply knowing that they have acted or responded with integrity. The sole reward for someone who is intrinsically motivated or self-directed may come from something like doing their very best or exceeding their best.

One method of motivation, however, is not necessarily better than another. You may notice a trend in what causes your *lack* of motivation in certain work or study areas. For example, you are not motivated to work additional hours unless you are paid overtime. In college, you are highly motivated at the beginning of the semester, but feel like dropping some of the more demanding and less interesting courses by midterm. Sometimes, you may see that you are both intrinsically and extrinsically motivated. The point is that *you should clearly understand your own motivation.* When you are aware of the source of your motivation, you can turn up the juice as needed. You can reward yourself externally with something pleasurable or encourage yourself with positive, reinforcing thoughts as you meet challenging or difficult situations.

Happiness is that state of consciousness which proceeds from the achievement of one's values.

—AYN RAND

Your motivation to interact with others is also important to observe. Advertisers and sales people work to understand and manipulate what motivates people. For example, when a car salesperson asks questions about what type of car we are looking for, they are fishing for clues on how to make a sales pitch. They discover we are looking for a family car, low payments, or a sporty look. They want to know what will motivate someone to buy a car.

Not all motivation is pretty; for example, making an underhanded or critical remark can be motivated by jealousy or envy. When your bottom-line motivation is revealed, we often see the unattractive underbelly of our insecurities, fears, greed, or pride. Becoming aware of the source of your motivation takes clarity, courage, and maturity. Learning how to replace fear-based motivation with the inspiration to prevail, even in the face of extreme difficulties, is the foundation of integrity.

When we see what motivates others, then we have an insight into how we might direct their energy or attention. For example, as a supervisor or manager, it is necessary to keep employees interested in staying on task, following through with good service, and providing quality effort to the company. Like you, most people are more motivated by recognition, acknowledgment, and gratitude. When you understand the basis of your own motivation, you begin to develop insight into what will inspire others to be successful.

Student Perspective

MOTIVATION AND PRIORITIZING

As students, we are faced with the harsh reality that a day only contains 24 hours, and sometimes that doesn't seem like nearly enough. Many demands are placed on our time, attention, and energy, and we are burdened with the task of having to organize it all. Just when we are convinced that we have achieved

this elusive balance and effectively conquered our scheduling nightmares, a new opportunity arises. A friend calls and says she will pay you if you help her move this weekend. Your favorite English professor offers you a part-time job in the department. That prestigious honor society just asked you to become a member. The drama club could really use someone as talented as you to take the lead in the play. The top fraternity is hosting a party, sends you an invitation, and seems interested in you as a pledge. Any number of things can arise that require you to make a choice about how to expend your time and energy. Before making that choice, be sure you have carefully considered the situation.

You may really need the extra money you'll earn by helping your friend, but don't you have a chemistry exam to study for this weekend? A job in the English department sounds great, but can you really invest 20 hours a week to work the shifts? You would love to star in the school play, but it requires 50 hours of rehearsal time over the next 6 weeks and finals are coming. Can you really afford to take the opportunity? Do you have the time available to dedicate to a new responsibility? Can you follow up on your obligations? Will other areas of your life have to be sacrificed in order to do this? Is this something you really want?

All of these are questions you must ask yourself before taking on new activities or making choices that could affect the delicate balance of your time management. There is a huge price to pay for overextending yourself—your academic performance! There is an even higher price to pay if you cannot deliver on your commitments and you allow your personal integrity to be compromised.

REFLECTION QUESTIONS

Has there ever been a time when you promised to do something, but found that you could not follow through? What interfered with your motivation? How might you deal differently with the situation?

Try This

ACCOUNTING FOR MOTIVATION

In this exercise, you are asked to indicate intrinsic and extrinsic motivators for each listed action, as well as describe your underlying reason for each motivator. Space is provided for you to list other actions. Remember, *intrinsically* motivated actions are driven by inner principles, feelings, values, and beliefs. *Extrinsically* motivated actions are driven by external rewards such as money, grades, recognition, comfort, or pleasure. It is very likely that many actions have both intrinsic and extrinsic motivators.

ACTION	INTRINSIC	EXTRINSIC
Working 40 hours a week	I take pride in the quality of work I perform.	**Money**—I need money to pay my living expenses.
Walking my dog daily	**Compassion**—I know my dog enjoys getting outside after beingcooped up all day. **Exercise**—This is a daily practicein self-discipline for my ownwell-being.	**Exercise**—I have to lose five pounds so I look better in my jeans.
Donating to a charity		
Helping a friend move across town		
Completing an assignment early		
Joining a campus club		
Going out with friends to a party, club, or social event		
Providing excellent service to clients or customers		

TAKING INITIATIVE

Whenever we venture out of our comfort zone, we take a risk. We take risks when we change the way we have always done something or when we set out to do something we have never done before. There is a trade-off; with risks, there is always the possibility of failure; without risks, there is no possibility for growth.

Taking initiative is a type of risk. When we initiate, we risk rejection, correction, or outright failure. The first step is usually the most difficult and taking initiative requires courage and confidence. Because those who take initiative can find themselves propelled into a leadership position, they should be prepared to take responsibility for the outcome. Taking initiative is usually highly valued in the workplace. Employees who make the company shine by going the extra mile or doing what has to be done to take customer service to the next level are usually well rewarded in the long run. A word of caution—initiative can quickly lose integrity when something is started and never finished. Initiating is not acting with integrity unless there is responsible follow through.

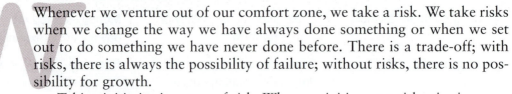

Try This

BREAKING BARRIERS TO INITIATIVE

Part A

Taking initiative often means making the first move. In a traditional classroom situation, students who raise their hands to answer questions are taking initiative. When we see things that must be done and our first response is to do it, then we take initiative. Here are a few scenarios designed to help you consider whether you are willing to take initiative.

Scenario One. It is a rainy day and you are sitting in a coffee shop. A man rushes in from the street and slips on the wet tiles, taking a nasty fall. His briefcase springs open and papers fly everywhere. You see his cell phone slide under the service counter. As he hits the floor, his body goes limp and he lays there motionless. Even though there are dozens of other people in the shop, you're sure you are the only one observing all of this at the moment. What is your most likely response?

A. Yell, "Somebody call 911." Then leave the shop for a more peaceful scene.

B. Jump up and see if the man is OK and then call 911.

C. Wait and see what happens next.

D. Help pick up the papers once somebody else starts to do it.

E. Point out where the cell phone is under the counter.

F. Other: _____

Scenario Two.   You work in a store that has a neon "Open" sign in the front window. To turn the light for the sign on and off, you have to get a ladder from the back storage area. When you come in for your evening shift you see that the open sign is not turned on. Before clocking in, you would:

A. Yell at the counter clerk, "Hey you forgot to turn the "open" sign on today!" and go clock in.

B. Go straight to the storage area, get the ladder, and turn the sign on before clocking in.

C. Go clock in secretly hoping you will have fewer customers if the sign stays off.

D. Other: _____

Part B

Review your answers and reflect on any real-life situations where you had the option to take initiative or make the first move. Unless you answered B for both scenarios and feel confident that your ability to take initiative is unrestricted, move to the next part of this exercise, which asks you to evaluate the barriers that might keep you from taking initiative.

For Scenario One, what are some of the reasons why you would or would not be the first one to directly respond to the man unconscious on the floor?

_____

_____

For Scenario Two, what are some of the reasons why you would or would not go back, get the ladder, and turn the sign on first?

_____

_____

In your real-life situations, what is the main factor that stops you from taking initiative?

_____

_____

What might be a first step in taking initiative more often?

_____

_____

ALIGNING WITH VALUES AND INTENTIONS

When you act with integrity, you bring values and goals into your moment-to-moment decision-making process. Your actions are intentional and purposeful, and they predictably align with your own code of ethics. Personal integrity is compromised when you lose sight of your intentions and become sidetracked or thrown off balance. An *intention can be compared to a motivational thought* that you hold in mind as you encounter challenging or new experiences. For example, a *value* is that you respect your elders, and your goal is to have a respectful interaction as you go into a meeting with a supervisor who is 10 years your senior. You hold the *intention* to be respectful even when you might disagree.

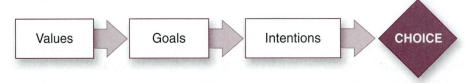

Values ➡ Goals ➡ Intentions ➡ CHOICE

Typically, we are not aware of our *intentions* (motivational thoughts that align with our goals) when we speak to someone. The words come out of our mouths before we have time to consider or edit our comments. There may be no thought given to the remarks we make. It is even more difficult to monitor our intentions when we are in emotional situations. For example, if you are out of sorts with a friend, you may make a sarcastic remark that's totally out of alignment with your intention to be kind to your companions. The question is, "What is the real intention underlying the remarks you made?" Are they mindless, automatic responses or is the true intention to be hurtful? If your intention is to be kind, then practice speaking kindly. The level of commitment, consistency, and follow through you bring to your intentions is a good measure of the quality of integrity you are capable of achieving.

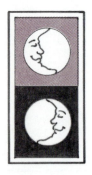

For Your Journal

Companion Website

CLARIFYING INTENTIONS

*Please respond to the following in your journal or by using the **Journal Module** on the CW.*

The objective of this journal is to be clear in your intentions before you speak in an emotionally charged situation. Within the next day or two, you may have the opportunity to observe how you respond to someone you are irritated by or disagree with.

Set an intention right now that will honor a principle of forgiveness. When the situation arises, make an honest effort to stick to your intention to be forgiving. Write about how this experiment unfolds for you. What do you think might happen differently if you are not able to apply your intention?

Courage is the ability to do what needs to be done, regardless of the cost or risk. Integrity is the ability to do the right thing, no matter what the doubts or temptations.

—CHRISTOPHER HOEING

Student Perspective

SELF-RESPONSIBILITY AND INTEGRITY

College is a place full of opportunities for achievement. Around every corner is a chance to try something new, compete for some recognition, and gain new experiences. Every class is an opportunity to expand your knowledge of the world around you. Every day is a new chance to find a way to grow. Just by being in school, you have earned the distinctive privilege of being among the minority of people who are striving to reach new heights of personal success. Look how far you have come already! And everything you now possess, you have earned for yourself through your efforts and hard work!

Now, when I say everything, that is exactly what I mean: everything you possess has been earned. There are two sides to this coin, however. That great new scholarship, the high placement test scores, that fabulous GPA, the respect and admiration of your peers—these are all earned. That horrible relationship, failed class, bad reputation, low self-esteem, fear of failure, lost opportunities, poor grades—these are also earned. Just as surely as you can work hard and achieve anything you desire in life, you can just as certainly earn the things you don't want. It is all about self-responsibility and the commitment you make or do not make to yourself. It is all about your sense of integrity.

When you are successful on a test, for example, it is usually easy to see that no one simply "handed" you a good score—you studied, worked hard, and earned that grade. You can easily identify the steps that you took to earn what you wanted. It is not as easy, however, to see this same connection when it comes to failures and misfortunes. Often, students blame the professor for putting material on the exam that was too hard; blame classmates for being disruptive and making it impossible to concentrate; or blame the telephone, TV, or family members for disrupting study time. This is not just an ineffective approach—it is also a case of self-sabotage! You did not disenfranchise yourself and give up the credit for doing well on that exam—so why do you think it is any more appropriate to relinquish responsibility when things go poorly? You owe it to yourself to take all of the credit (yes, credit) for failing. When you accept the responsibility, you can identify the steps you took to earn the failure. Then, you can take the necessary action to consciously make the changes that will help you avoid future failures because you now know what not to do.

REFLECTION QUESTIONS

Has there ever been a time that you blamed someone for something you did wrong? How did this affect your situation? How might the outcome have changed had you taken responsibility for what happened?

Accountability

Self-responsibility means being accountable. Accountability is a quality of leadership. When we have more authority, we also take on more responsibility. We are accountable first to ourselves, meaning we carefully consider commitments or promises *before* we make them. We are also accountable for aligning our values and goals with our choices and behaviors.

Before making commitments and obligations, you should *honestly assess your ability to keep your word and offer it only if there is a sincere willingness to follow through.* Integrity is where self-awareness and self-regulation are integrated. It takes honest self-awareness to know if you are making a commitment you can truly keep. For example, before promising to attend a meeting on a day that you usually have a standing commitment to work out at the gym, consider which use of your time is in closer alignment with your values. If the meeting is not required by work or is not something you are directly interested in, you may want to decline the invitation or say, "This sounds like a great meeting, but I have a standing commitment at that time." If you say, "Sure, I will try to make the meeting," you are not really being honest with yourself or the other person because you already know there is something else you will do at that time.

Sometimes, we get in the habit of tentatively agreeing to do things that we really do not have the time or interest in doing. Friends, coworkers, and companions quickly find out that we are unreliable when we cancel or fail to show up at times we casually, and thoughtlessly, agreed to.

Self-regulation applies to how you might carefully monitor what you say. This means you do not say things you do not mean or allow yourself to do things that interfere with the promises you have made. When you are accountable to this degree, there is no excuse or hiding from the truth if the promise is not carried out. Self-responsibility requires admitting when you have failed and not looking for ways to blame circumstances or others. Instead, a fearless acknowledgment that you missed the mark keeps integrity intact.

Trustworthiness

Integrity is something we learn from experience. We learn that in order to respect ourselves and for others to respect us, we must be worthy of trust. We do our very best to tell the truth, and we do not mislead. Only *you* know if you truly succeed in being honest and trustworthy. Trustworthiness is an attribute that is earned over time. We may be trustworthy in our own eyes, but others only know this by our consistent actions. Our personal efforts to act with integrity in the face of all the failings of society are necessary not only for our own success, but also for the balance and well-being of the world.

Student Perspective

SELF-RESPONSIBILITY

At this stage of my life, I have come to understand that for me, "success" is a reflection of self-motivation, self-awareness, responsibility, and resilience; it is not merely something that just "happens." For me, success is a holistic and inclusive set of ideals that encompasses every aspect of my life. It really doesn't matter whether I win or lose; the benefit gained from any life circumstance comes in the form of the lesson I learn in the process and the improvement I make in myself because of it. I have found that as long as I remain true to myself, aware of what I feel, and honest in my efforts, I always succeed, even if I don't get exactly what I want. The keys are not being afraid to keep trying and knowing how to use what I learn from my failures to make better choices and get to the successes.

I have learned that sound decisions about the world and choices about my life cannot be made unless intellect is tempered with intuition and knowledge is balanced by wisdom. With this comes the knowledge that everything I do must be tempered with empathy, maturity, responsibility, and self-knowledge in order to be of any real value. These attributes are unique because they are acquired through individual life experience—they cannot be learned from any book, teacher, or guru. I have needed all of my problems, misfortunes, and mistakes in order to get where I am today and to become the person I have grown into. I consider each new insight I gain into my own emotions and each new personal connection I make to the world around me to be of great importance in my day-to-day life. These are the things that I find to be my most valuable and fulfilling achievements because they help me adapt to my environment, communicate with others, and understand my circumstances. I have learned how to solve problems, build relationships, and achieve my goals, not through special aptitudes, but through the ability to accept responsibility for everything that goes on in my life and to learn from difficult situations—not let them beat me. Success, in this manner, has no name or shape—it exists in the simple ability to grow as a person with each life experience and to keep on going no matter what.

SUMMARY

Integrity is an attribute of character that includes being trustworthy and accountable. It means being **self-motivated** and being aware of what motivates us. Some motivation is internal and results from our principles and values. This is called *intrinsic* motivation. When we are motivated by external rewards, such as money or grades, this is called *extrinsic* motivation. When we can understand our own sources of motivation, we can better work to motivate others. When we see something that must be done and we do it, we are taking **initiative**. Once we initiate something, we also take responsibility for following through and seeing things to completion.

We act with integrity when we consider our principles and values by making our intentions clear. An **intention** is like a motivational thought that we hold in mind when making decisions. The level of commitment we bring to our intentions is a good measure of the quality of integrity we are capable of achieving.

Accountability means we are responsible to others and ourselves for our actions and words. We don't make promises we can't keep. *Self-regulation* is used to monitor our words and keep us from saying things we don't really mean or cannot possibly do. **Trustworthiness** is earned by our ability to be consistently honest and reliable.

Case Studies

CASE STUDY 6.1

Accountability

Diego is working full-time at an information technology firm. His primary duties include backing up the systems to tape in the evenings. Both he and his coworker, Fran, have been with the company for over three years. The firm has invested a great deal of trust in both Diego and Fran—the back-up tape procedure is a high security task. If there is any failure in a tape back-up, it could cost the company millions of dollars, literally overnight.

Diego and Fran have always had a great working relationship and stay in very close contact by cell phone. They take their jobs very seriously and have always acted with great integrity when it comes to taking time off. They have worked out a way to handle the division of responsibilities so that if one of them needs the night off or takes sick leave, the other covers the shift.

Fran asked Diego to cover a shift for her so she can attend her sister's wedding reception dinner. On the way to work, Diego gets a call from his neighbor who tells him that his house has been robbed and the police are trying to reach him. As he turns around to head home, he tries to reach Fran on her cell phone and beeper. When there is no answer, he leaves a message. When he reaches his house, he sees that things are a huge mess. All of his stereo electronics and computers were stolen. Diego is really upset. He decides he cannot go to work with this situation going on. Around midnight, he tries Fran again on her cell phone and gets no answer. Diego is so devastated that he cannot think straight. He has a passing thought about calling his boss, but it's after 1:30 A.M. Finally, he doses off around 3 A.M. The next day, Diego is awakened by a phone call from his highly irate boss who lets him know he is fired.

REFLECTION QUESTIONS

1. Considering the circumstances, should Diego be held accountable for not calling in or coming to work after years of reliable service to the firm?

2. Should Fran be held accountable for not checking her messages or returning calls on a night off?

3. What was the main factor that influenced Diego's decision not to go to work?

4. In your opinion, was there a failure of integrity?

CASE STUDY 6.2

Procrastination

Tonya is a college teacher at the local community college. She is attending graduate school at night to finish her master's degree. Because she also works full-time during the day, her schedule is very demanding. Each weekend, she has to set aside an average of 10 hours to read or write for her graduate courses. Tonya has been in the evening program for two years and because she has also taken a full load in the summer, she only has one more semester to graduate.

All her courses must be taken in sequence, so she must complete each course with a C or better to move to the next level. If she fails to complete a course, she loses out on taking the next semester and must wait a year to take the class over.

Half way into the semester Tonya's department chair at the college encourages her to take on a community service project for her social science classes during two weekends the next month. Without thinking, Tonya agrees. Later, she talks with a friend who invites her to play golf the coming weekend. Thinking she needs a break, Tonya promises to join her on Sunday. On Saturday, Tonya wakes up and sees that the yard looks shabby. It's a beautiful fall day, so Tonya spends about six hours working in the yard. By evening, she is exhausted, so she watches TV and goes to sleep early. She has a great golf game the next day and is starting to feel more relaxed about writing her final paper for a course.

The next two weekends, Tonya is tied up with the community service project. With only two weeks left in the semester, she promises to make time the next weekend to begin her paper. To clear the time on the weekend, she puts herself in overdrive and cleans the entire house, runs all of her errands, and stays up late to answer student e-mails. She finds she is not sleeping well at night because she is worried about not finishing the paper. For two days, she forgets to eat lunch and breakfast because she is so busy.

Tonya is out of time and has to start her final paper this weekend. She wakes up on Saturday morning with a terrible case of the flu. Nothing gets done on the paper.

REFLECTION QUESTIONS

1. Outline all of the choices Tonya made that might qualify as procrastination and kept her from writing the paper.
2. At which point did Tonya lose sight of her intention to make time to write the paper on the weekend?
3. At which point did Tonya make an effort to create the time on the weekend?
4. How did Tonya's efforts to make time on the weekend backfire on her?
5. Do you think Tonya's illness has anything to do with procrastination? Why or why not?
6. If Tonya acted with complete integrity, how would her choices be different?

Demonstration of Competency

*Please respond to the following in your journal or by using the **Demonstration of Competency Module** on the CW.*

One aspect of integrity is mindfulness. Mindfulness means being present or being aware of what is happening now—both inwardly and outwardly. Mindfulness also means not doing things "just any old way" or "the same old way." Make every effort your best effort. When you are mindful, you work with clear attention and intention while maintaining a state of quietude. From this position you see and experience the world through new eyes and senses.

For your demonstration of competency, practice mindfulness as a method of maintaining and growing integrity. Native American lore tells the story about the wise man who holds his words on his tongue seven times before sending them out into the world. This means there is an effort to reflect on or be mindful of what is said. By holding the words on his tongue, there is an inner observation of the words, the underlying intentions, and the potential impact on those who hear them.

Make a commitment to practice this type of mindfulness for one day by making your intentions very clear to yourself and considering your words before you speak, especially in emotionally charged situations. Write about your experiences and examine whether or not you were successful.

Additional references and resources for chapter topics can be found at **www.prenhall.com/gray**.

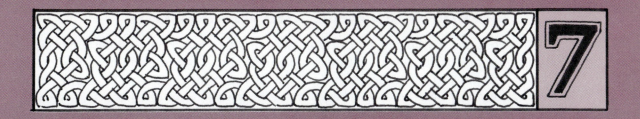

Integration

TIME AND LEARNING

Time is the coin of your life. It is the only coin you have, and only you can determine how it will be spent. Be careful lest you let other people spend it for you.

—CARL SANDBURG (1878–1967)

Self-directed learners make the time necessary to ensure the quality of their learning experiences. What you choose to make time for shows the real priorities that are directing your life. Once you master being a self-directed learner, you are in control of your choices, energy, attention, and how you utilize your time. Noticing how you talk about time can make you more aware of how you use your time. Planning and prioritizing are two keys to saving time. When you learn to balance your time between work and play, you are better able to make time for everything.

 ## What If . . .

What if you had all of the time necessary to do everything you want to do? Can you imagine a situation where you might have too much time?

SPENDING, KILLING, AND MAKING TIME

Consider the language you typically use when referring to your time. Do you talk about spending time or making time? More importantly, what criteria do you use to decide how to spend your time each day? By answering questions like these, you begin to see how your view of time affects what you do with your time. In other words, the language and thoughts you use to refer to time begin to direct how time is perceived and applied in your life. Your answers also reveal what is truly important to you. When you honestly evaluate how you are actually spending your time, you see exactly why you get what you do out of life.

It is revealing to examine the meaning of different descriptive phrases used regarding time. Notice that when you say, "I always make time for that," you imply that creating time is necessary to maintain something valuable. For example, you *make* time for your friends and family, but you *spend* time studying or watching TV. The phrase *spending time* can be viewed exactly as it sounds—you pay for your life experiences with moments of time. How you choose to spend your time is how you are expending your life. When you spend time, you spend your life. You may have heard people say, "I spent over 50 hours at work this week," or "I am spending way too much time worrying about this relationship." Spending time seems to imply overextending or paying too high a cost.

On another scale, you *kill time*—waiting for something or playing a computer game. You tend to kill time when you have no specific goals or agendas. Killing time can also be viewed as letting life pass you by while you idle away at unproductive and insignificant absorptions. You also *take* time, or *steal a few hours,* for yourself, once in a while to relax, enjoy life, and participate in something pleasurable. Noticing how you speak about time increases your awareness of what you do with your time. This can be one method of checking to see if your priorities are in order with your goals.

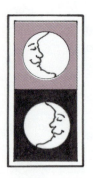

For Your Journal

SPEAKING OF TIME

*Please respond to the following in your journal or by using the **Journal Module** on the CW.*

Finish the following sentences.

In any given week, I spend most of my time _____

I enjoy passing time with _____

If I am killing time, I am usually _____

I always make time for _____

In my spare time, I like to _____

I plan to create time for _____

I could spend less time _____

The biggest waste of time is _____

I lose time when I _____

I want to find time to _____

One way to make extra time is to _____

The best use of my time is when I _____

It takes too much time to _____

What are your top three priorities in life?

_____

_____

_____

Write a brief summary of how your priorities are connected (or not) to how you speak about your time. What could you change to make more time for these three priorities?

BALANCING TIME

Students realize that they have to *make time* to study and that teachers have planned homework that takes almost all of their time. These are indeed the expectations of college life when you are a full-time student. Add to this work, family, friends, chores, and errands, and you have a recipe for burnout.

If you haven't experienced burnout, it is what occurs if you spend too much time trying to do too much. What tends to happen is that you lose interest and energy. You can even run yourself into the ground to the extent that you get physically ill. Balancing your time among work, play, study, rest, and people is probably the most formidable challenge you will meet in college life.

A key to balancing your time is to find creative ways to *make time* for everything. This may sound contradictory, but what it means is planning.

You make time, intentionally, by planning for work, study, play, friends, *and distractions*. Keeping your plans flexible by building in *empty time* helps you keep your sanity. For example, plan on at least two to three hours of empty time per day so you can goof off, rest, exercise, or check your e-mail. This may seem outrageous if you already don't have enough time; however, one way or another, you lose two to three hours a day to distractions, confusion, emotional upset, low energy, and small unplanned tasks. You also lose time to events or people that sidetracked you. When you have a plan with empty time included, you can pause for a while and still get back on track quickly; in other words, you don't stay lost in the jungle of distractions.

The key to building in time for sidetracking is that it should not exceed 10 percent of your day. If you can keep your distractions down to 10 percent of your time, you will seriously reduce the number of hours you currently spend being sidetracked. By planning for distractions, you stay more aware of how much time is used on them. Also, building in empty time gives you the space to relax once in a while. Making time to recharge can often fall off your list of things to do, yet it is essential to your mental and physical well-being to stop and do something relaxing and enjoyable. Scheduling empty or recharge time helps you gain energy. The more energy you have, the better use you can make of all of your time. *Try planning your distractions intentionally as a purposeful recharge.*

Planning also means that you are setting an intention, or an aim, to make something specific happen. This is a powerful mode of creating time. When you set your plans with an emotional commitment, you are not only making time, but you are also creating the possibility for them to be actualized.

Student Perspective

MOTIVATION AND PRIORITIZING TIME

Most college programs require that you take several courses, sometimes five or six different subjects, all at the same time and keep up with all of them. It may seem at times that every professor assigns homework as if his or her class was the only one you are taking. They also don't seem to understand that students have lives outside college that also demand time and energy. They see absolutely nothing wrong with assigning 3 chapters to read and 10 pages of notes to write over 2 days. If you multiply those 3 chapters times the 5 classes you are taking, you have 2 days, 15 chapters, half a notebook of notes, and a partridge in a pear tree. You might be wondering if such a Herculean feat is humanly possible. Well, considering the fact that this is your education, your future, and your choice of classes and class load—you bet it is! Just get control of *how you will organize and spend your time* so that it all gets done.

It is a good practice to begin organizing by using a day planner or calendar to keep your assignments organized; that way, you won't forget anything. It is also important to understand your own likes, dislikes, weaknesses, and strengths—this makes a tremendous difference in how you approach the different subjects, when you should work on each one, and how quickly you can get through them. If, for example, you have math, science, and literature homework all due in the morning, and you enjoy literature the most, you should save that for last. Why? Because the other subjects will take more time and effort, so you want to make sure that they get adequate attention while your mind is sharpest. The subject you are most connected to is less difficult to approach, takes less time, and feels like "fun" after getting the harder stuff out of the way. On the other hand, if you have things planned that must get done in addition to your homework, like a doctor's appointment, then try to optimize your day by taking a lighter subject along with you to read during wait times. Save the more intensive material for later when all of your errands are done and you can really focus.

There are only 24 hours in a day, and when your workload is heavy, you must make a real effort to use those hours to your greatest advantage. Most importantly, put off the things that are least important until the most important things are finished. If there is a party this evening at 9 P.M., and at 8:45 you are still six pages short of finishing your English paper, you have a choice to make. Some things can wait and some can't. The idea here is to consciously set your priorities and try your best to organize your time to optimize each day.

REFLECTION QUESTIONS

How well do you prioritize your workload at present? Can you think of a time that you could not get everything done? What happened? How might you improve your management of time so that it all gets done and you still have free time?

Try This

PLANNING FOR EVERYTHING

Create a *plan for everything* for tomorrow. Fill in the hours and times below. Make sure you include two hours of empty time. Empty time can be broken out into 10- to 30-minute blocks. Consider booking your empty time as a buffer between larger events. Remember to schedule some recharge time in your day as well.

ACTIVITY	HOURS	TIME OF DAY/NIGHT*
Work		
Study		
Class		
People		
Empty time		
Sleep		
Driving		
Eating		
Recharge/relax		

*Total should equal 24 hours.

Try to stick to the plan—make your most firm and resolute commitment to follow through on this plan with all of your integrity. Note here the distractions or events that fill your empty time or get you sidetracked:

_____

_____

_____

Were any of the distractions preventable? Were any of the events unnecessary? If so, how will you prevent them in the future?

_____

_____

_____

SAVING TIME

Saving time means working efficiently, managing multiple tasks, and developing a good memory. Self-directed learners who can focus attention conserve their energy, minimizing distractions saves huge amounts of time. They are highly productive and single-minded and capable of making good use of time. They are motivated by their own personal goals, they prioritize, and they are willing to ask questions. Here are some examples of how the qualities of a self-directed learner make time more abundant.

QUALITIES OF A SELF-DIRECTED LEARNER	TIME SAVERS
Able to sustain focused attention	Remembers what is read; not rereading as much or as often
Adaptable	Finds creative ways to multitask and save time
Listens actively	Does not waste time on misunderstandings
Takes initiative	Knows what has to be done and does not wait to be told what to do and when
Asks questions	Clarifies instructions to save time and effort

When you save time, you remain flexible and more relaxed. Take a moment to think about how you might work more efficiently in your daily routines to conserve time.

Student Perspective

This book contains some of the most powerful, important, meaningful information you may ever find. You have, by now, read the little pieces I contributed throughout. You have been exposed to the ideas and tools that

can help you to take control of your life and start building your future, personality, and lifestyle in alignment with what you really want. But this is nothing more than a bunch of jargon and rhetoric unless you apply some of what you have read. You have wasted your time thumbing through this text if you are unable to find meaning in what it contains. I offer one final thought for you to ponder as you close the cover on this book: Can you be courageous enough to CHOOSE the "hard way"? I realize this may sound silly, but the key to your success or failure in life may depend on this one principle alone. Are you willing to be honest with yourself? Are you prepared to look at what you have created and truly see who you are? Can you decide what you truly want out of life? Are you ready and willing to make a conscious choice to face the obstacles that stand in your way? Are you prepared to accept this responsibility and embrace the awesome opportunities that stand before you?

It is *easy* to go through school, work, and LIFE on "autopilot," not really thinking about what, how, or why you do the things you do from day to day. It is *easy* to simply accept the "hard knocks" and "circumstances" that hold you back from what you truly want in life. It is *easy* to blame your parents, childhood, social caste, or economic background for the problems you face. Worst of all, it is *easy* to trick yourself into believing that you are content sitting where you are in life when deep in your heart, you yearn for so much more. All of these things are *easy*—they require little effort, offer little resistance, and save you the trouble of having to struggle. I know because I lived the "easy" way for years before I finally made the choice to accept responsibility for myself, my life, and my future. I can attest to the fact that the "easy way" doesn't get you what you want or help bring you to where you want to be. Only courage can do that. Only the willingness to face your life head on, accept responsibility, and take action can do that. Only your own power to choose can get you started toward your dreams, and only your will to succeed will make it happen. The "easy way" will keep you stuck in the position you are in. The "easy way" will build a wall between you and everything you ever wanted in life by allowing your future to be decided by everything and everyone else—the "easy way" doesn't really care what you want. It took me years to figure that out—I hope the lesson comes quicker for you.

It may surprise you to know, after reading in the introduction about how well I am doing in school and how much I have accomplished, that I was a high school dropout. I had my first child at the age of 16. I was married and divorced by the time I was 18—alone and raising two young children without the benefit of even a high school diploma. At minimum wage, I worked two—sometimes three—jobs to keep my bills paid and children fed. I made one mistake after another—and not once in those 20 years had I ever stopped and considered the fact that it was all my doing. Not once in my life did I even come close to accepting that all of the misfortunes and struggles were the result of my actions and choices. I blamed my parents for "messing up my life" when I was too young to take care of myself. I blamed my first husband for tricking me into marriage and mistreating me. I blamed society for discriminating against young mothers, and the economy for keeping people like me from getting ahead in life. I blamed my boss when I got fired from one job because the city bus was running late (then, I blamed the bus driver). I blamed my landlord for my apartment being so run down. I continued to go on this way—living in a world where everyone else was to blame for my unhappiness—until one day, I was sitting alone in my run-down little apartment filled with garage-sale furnishings looking for a new job. I had the classified section open to the "hotel/restaurant" page, and as I read the listings for waitresses (all I was qualified to do), it struck me—I was alone. It wasn't just the empty apartment: I was really alone. No one else in the world was there to find me a new job. No one else could keep my bills paid. No one else could fix the problems I was facing. No one else had to look in the mirror and see my face—except for me. All of those people who had come through my life were gone now. All of the events that caused me pain were in the past. My friends and family did not have to live my life—I did. The world around me did not care that I felt cheated and alone. It didn't care that I was angry and hurt. It didn't care that I felt I deserved more out of life. It was not going to bend the rules for me or hand me a life jacket just because I thought I needed one. If things were going to get any better, I had to do it myself.

I was horrified! A second realization occurred just then—more terrifying than the first. When I cut out of chemistry in 9th grade to go out to lunch with my friends and ended up failing, that was MY choice, not the result of peer pressure. When I became sexually active and got pregnant instead of taking precautions, that was MY choice, not the result of being pushed into it. When I packed my bags and left home instead of finishing school, that was MY choice, not the result of my dysfunctional family. When I got married, that was MY choice, not something I was forced to do in order to be more socially accepted. When I got stuck in one crappy job after another, those were MY choices, not the result of some unfair, cruel world trying to keep me down.

It suddenly became clear to me—after all those years—that there was no one to hold accountable for my life but me. There may have been circumstances that made things hard for me, people who influenced my choices and behaviors, and events that I had no control over, but at the root of everything was one simple fact—in every instance, I chose how to respond and I acted—period. I was the one who decided my own cruel fate without really thinking my choices through or considering alternatives. I had not yet accepted that responsibility, so I got stuck with what life handed me because of all those years on autopilot. I realized in that moment sitting over the newspaper that what I had gotten was not at all what I wanted.

But what should have been an empowering realization for me was instead a terrifying discovery. Because I finally understood that I was the cause of my struggles and failures, I was then stuck with the task of also accepting responsibility for cleaning it all up. That was about seven years ago, and I am still working to achieve my goals and realign my life with my values and aspirations. There was no miraculous, immediate outward change in my life. The change occurred inside of me—I had resolved to take responsibility and stop blaming the world for my problems. I focused on building a future, planning an education, striving for a career . . . one step at a time. My life circumstances were not going to make the process easy for me, but I have never faltered in my determination to succeed. I not only accepted, but also actually embraced the "hard way" and really started working for what I wanted. That year, I ended the bad relationship I was in and spent some time alone, learning about myself, re-determining my values, and becoming comfortable with my new sense of self-reliance and responsibility. The year after, I focused on trying to save money to move out of that apartment. It would be another two years before I reached the point of being ready to get my GED and start college. The rest is history.

It has been—and still is—difficult, but I never considered giving up. Life is far too short, and there are so many wonderful things to experience that I absolutely refuse to be cheated out of my dreams. I refuse to be my own nemesis. I would rather work twice as hard as everyone else if it means I get what I want in the end. The thoughts of "if only I had . . ." are all gone now. I removed "should have," "could have," and "ought to have" from my vocabulary entirely. There are no regrets or guilt. Each and every bad choice, stupid decision, mistake, and failure has become part of who I am, and they have all helped me to grow and learn. Of course, I realize now that I could have saved myself many years of struggling if I had just figured all this out a bit sooner. I had to discover the keys all on my own, and it has been a really rough ride; a ride that I would not wish on anyone.

You are not in the position I was in. You have been given the most wonderful opportunity—you are holding the answers in your hand right now. You don't have to suffer and struggle to figure it all out. You don't have to waste years of your life getting nowhere and feeling bad about yourself. You don't have to spend years more repairing the damage. You are empowered—right now. You have the answers—right now. Not another day need to go by that you are not in control of your life. Not one more minute should pass that you don't feel good about who you are, where you are going, and how you will get there. You have it all right here. Now, the choice is yours—will it be the "easy way" or are you ready to start working for what you want out of life? I think you are worth the extra effort, and I hope you take what we have provided here and do amazing things with your life. There is no time like the present—so get started!

For Your Journal

YOUR RESPONSE

*Please respond to the following in your journal or by using the **Journal Module** on the CW.*

Write about how you relate to the experience in the preceding Student Perspective. Do you have an inspirational story from your life that you can share?

SUMMARY

What you do with your time is the most revealing indicator of your actual ability to integrate goals with choices. When you honestly evaluate how you are actually spending your time, you see exactly why you get what you do out of life.

Some suggestions for good time management include:

- Use your critical-thinking skills to align your long-term goals with your decisions about how to allocate your time in any given day.
- Examine whether or not your activities for the day contain balanced time. Are you making time for everything?
- Make time for your priorities every day.
- Keep your distractions down to 10 percent of your time.
- Make time to recharge every day.
- Saving time means working efficiently, managing multiple tasks, and developing a good memory.

When you set your plans with an emotional commitment, you are making time and creating the possibility that they will be actualized.

Case Studies

CASE STUDY 7.1

Avoiding Burnout

Raul has worked 40 hours a week for a national package delivery service for over 3 years. He is making good money; in fact, he has saved about 20 percent of his earnings from each paycheck and has enough cash to pay for 2 years of college and a new sports car. It is his second semester at college. He attends full-time at night and on weekends. Raul is also engaged to be married in the summer. Although his fiancée understands that he has returned to college so he can upgrade his career possibilities, there is a strain on the relationship because he can only see her on Sunday evenings. Raul decides to try to graduate quicker by taking two on-line courses in addition to the evening and weekend classes. The classes are very demanding and he is about to either drop or fail them if something doesn't change in the next week. Raul is exhausted all of the time while at work—he is stressed and irritable. Because his job involves driving, he cannot afford to have a careless or angry moment that could cause an accident. His fiancée is losing patience because he has not seen her for two weekends. He also has a terrible cold that makes it hard for him to think straight. He calls his best friend to help him out with some advice on how to prevent being totally overwhelmed.

REFLECTION QUESTIONS

1. If you were Raul's best friend, what first steps would you suggest he consider to save himself from total burnout?
2. How could Raul keep his job, pass the on-line courses, and save his relationship?
3. What are some financial options Raul could consider to immediately make his life easier?
4. What are some time management and planning options for Raul so he does not end up in this situation again next semester?

CASE STUDY 7.2

Saving Time

Kita has two children age two and five. She is a single mother who relies on her parents to baby-sit so she can go to college four nights a week. Kita also

INTEGRATION   141

works 40 hours a week. She uses her weekends to study and get errands and housework done. Using the following list of tasks that Kita has to accomplish in 48 hours, see if you can suggest how she might work efficiently and manage or overlap multiple tasks. The objective is to save time so she can relax and enjoy a few extra hours with her children over the weekend.

Return phone calls (1 hour)

Answer classmate e-mail about course work (2 hours)

Outline a paper (2 hours)

Do laundry (2 hours)

Wash dishes (1 hour)

Read three chapters (3 hours)

Review notes for test (2 hours)

Grocery shopping (2 hours)

Research paper topic on the Internet (2 hours)

Buy more printer ink (1 hour)

Cook and eat nine meals (three meals a day) (10 hours)

Sleep for seven hours a night (20 hours)

What strategies can Kita use to minimize distractions or sidetracking during this time?

Demonstration of Competency

*Please respond to the following in your journal or by using the **Demonstration of Competency Module** on the CW.*

The demonstration of competency in this chapter is a self-assessment that provides you with feedback on the core competencies and student success skill sets covered in this textbook. It is important to honestly identify your barriers to student success skills, such as focusing attention, maintaining well-being, and sustaining motivation. Knowing more about your personal challenges and strengths in the four core competencies will provide you with powerful information to guide your efforts in making conscious choices and becoming a receptive, self-directed learner.

In some cases, this book made you aware of areas where you need to improve. This might make you rate your skills lower than what you previously thought they were, which is not necessarily a bad thing. It just means that you are now able to more accurately assess yourself. Based on your own ratings, you are offered suggestions to deepen your efforts in areas where you feel you still need the greatest improvement. These suggestions should be augmented by your own exploration of additional resources.

Although this book offers many valuable ideas to help you discover how to make conscious choices and become a more self-directed learner, it does not propose to resolve all of the barriers to the learning or thinking process. Eliminating deep-set barriers to learning receptivity is beyond the scope of this textbook and often requires the expertise of professionals in specific cognitive or health-related fields.

Instructions: Rate yourself on the following student success skill sets. The most valuable result of this assessment will be an awareness of your strengths and weaknesses. From this awareness you can continue your self-directed learning process and reach your goals.

STUDENT SUCCESS SKILLS	RATING
Rating Scale 1 = I am a star 2 = I could do better 3 = I need major improvement	
CRITICAL THINKING	
Before I make decisions, I consider how various factors will influence my choices.	
I frequently examine the source of my beliefs and opinions to determine their ongoing validity.	
I can respect and acknowledge beliefs and opinions that are different from or conflict with my own.	
I am not afraid to ask questions or request assistance.	
I am open to learning new things and willing to find different ways to do things.	
Total Points	
MOTIVATION	
I clearly understand my personal values.	
I prioritize my time and energy based on my personal goals.	
I am not afraid to take the initiative.	
I am aware of the primary source of my motivation.	

I know how to minimize procrastination.	
Total Points	
COMPREHENSION	
I know how to sustain my focus and concentrate on what I am doing.	
I am in control of my responses to inner and outer distractions.	
I observe details accurately.	
I can remember information and concepts.	
I can apply what I learn to real-life or abstract situations.	
Total Points	
SELF-MASTERY	
I am mindful of my actions and my thoughts are self-reflective.	
I am trustworthy and accountable for my words and actions.	
I have good self-esteem.	
I practice healthy living through my choices of what I take into my body and senses.	
I am flexible, resilient, and adaptable to change in my life or living environment.	
Total Points	

Record the total points for each core competency:

Critical Thinking = _____ (max 15)   Comprehension = _____ (max 15)

Motivation   = _____ (max 15)   Self-Mastery   = _____ (max 15)

Grand total for all competencies = _____ (max 60 points/min 20 points)

Overall Score

60–55 This rating indicates that you feel you have an excellent grasp of all of the concepts in this textbook. You will continue to benefit by practicing what you have learned in real-life situations. You are encouraged to share your knowledge and experience with friends and classmates. Plan on extending your competencies by reviewing the additional resources on the website or asking your instructor for suggestions.

54–45 This rating shows you have a basic confidence in your student success skills. There are a few specific areas where you feel you need improvement, but in most areas, you appear to be very comfortable with your abilities. You can locate more resources for specific competencies or skills you wish to strengthen on the website or you may ask your instructor for suggestions.

44–31 This rating shows you have to focus your efforts on improving several of your competencies. You should work diligently to upgrade your skills in order to keep up with the standards expected of successful students in higher education. Review the contents of this book for more ideas on improving. Also, discuss your concerns with your instructor. A visit to your academic counselor's office should be helpful. You can locate more resources for specific competencies or skills you wish to strengthen on the website.

30–20 This rating shows that you feel serious and immediate improvement is definitely needed in all of the competencies for student success. Review the contents of this book for more ideas on improving. Also, discuss your concerns with your instructor. Make an appointment to speak with someone in the academic counseling or guidance office at your college. The counseling office knows of additional resources and courses that could be very helpful in improving your skills. You can locate more resources for specific competencies or skills you wish to strengthen on the website.

Additional references and resources for chapter topics can be found at **www.prenhall.com/gray**.

References

CHAPTER 1 Self-Directed Learning

Dobson, J. C. (2001). *Thirty-eight values to live by.* Nashville, TN: W Publishing Group.

Lewis, H. (2000). *A question of values: Six ways we make the personal choices that shape our lives.* Mt. Jackson, VA: Axios Press.

Simon, S. B., Howe, L. W., & Kirschenbaum, H. (1995). *Values clarification* (rev. ed.). New York: Warner Books.

Smith, H. W. (2000). *What matters most: The power of living your values.* New York: Fireside.

Stepahin, J. M. (2000). *Personal values: The application of personal values to the world of work.* Klamath Falls, OR: Pacific Press.

Watson, D. L. & Tharp, R. G. (1997). *Self-directed behavior: Self-modification for personal adjustment.* Pacific Grove, CA: Brooks & Cole.

Young, A. (2000). *Life lessons my mother taught me: Universal values from extraordinary times.* Los Angeles, CA: J. P. Tarcher.

CHAPTER 2 Choices

Arrow, K. J. (1970). *Social choice and individual values* (2nd ed.). New Haven, CT: Yale University Press.

Beattie, M. (2002). *Choices: Taking control of your life and making it matter.* San Francisco, CA: HarperCollins.

Fox, E. (1992). *Find and use your inner power.* San Francisco, CA: HarperCollins.

Glasser, W. (1998). *Choice theory in the classroom* (rev. ed.). New York: Perennial.

Glasser, W. (1999). *Choice theory: A new psychology of personal freedom.* New York: Perennial.

Glasser, W. & Glasser, C. (1999). *The language of choice theory.* New York: HarperCollins.

Grabhorn, L. (2000). *Excuse me, your life is waiting: The astonishing power of feelings.* Charlottesville, VA: Hampton Roads.

Hastie, R. & Dawes, R. M. (2001). *Rational choice in an uncertain world: The psychology of judgment and decision making*. Thousand Oaks, CA: Sage.

Peale, N. V. (1996). *The power of positive thinking*. New York: Ballantine.

Robbins, A. (1997). *Unlimited power: The new science of personal achievement*. New York: Fireside.

Schelling, T. C. (1985). *Choice and consequence: Perspectives of an errant economist*. Cambridge, MA: Harvard University Press.

Wilde, S. (1996). *Infinite self: Thirty-three steps to reclaiming your inner power*. Carlsbad, CA: Hay House.

CHAPTER 3 Attention

Adler, B. (1988). *The student's memory book*. New York: Doubleday.

Amen, D. G. (2001). *Healing ADD: The breakthrough program that allows you to see and heal the six types of ADD*. New York: Putnam.

Barkley, R. A. (2000). *Taking charge of ADHD: The complete, authoritative guide for parents* (rev. ed.). New York: Guilford.

Bodian, S. (1999). *Meditation for dummies*. New York: Wiley.

Browning, W. G. (1997). *Memory power for exams*. Foster City, CA: Cliffs Notes.

Buksbazen, J. D. & Matthiessen, P. (2002). *Zen meditation in plain English*. Somerville, MA: Wisdom.

Buzan, T. (1991). *Use both sides of your brain*. New York: E. P. Dutton.

Canfield, J., Hewitt, L., & Hansen, M. V. (2000). *The power of focus*. Edison, NJ: Health Communications.

Csikszentmihalyi, M. (1990). *Flow*. New York: Harper & Row.

Duncan, S. (2001). *Present moment awareness*. Novato, CA: New World Library.

Goleman, D. P. (1997). *Emotional intelligence*. New York: Bantam.

Hallowell, E. M. & Ratey, J. J. (1995). *Driven to distraction: Recognizing and coping with attention deficit disorder from childhood through adulthood*. Westport, CT: Touchstone.

Herrmann, D. J. (1993). *Improving student memory*. Seattle, WA: Hogrefe & Huber.

Kabat-Zinn, J. (1995). *Wherever you go, there you are: Mindfulness meditation in everyday life*. New York: Hyperion.

Kelly, K. & Ramundo, P. (1996). *You mean I'm not lazy, stupid, or crazy?!: A self-help book for adults with attention deficit disorder*. New York: Fireside.

Mooney, J. & Cole, D. (2000). *Learning outside the lines: Two ivy league students with learning disabilities and ADHD give you the tools for academic success and educational revolution.* New York: Fireside.

Murphy, K. R. & Levert, S. (1995). *Out of the fog: Treatment options and coping strategies for adult attention deficit disorder.* New York: Hyperion.

Solden, S. (1995). *Women with attention deficit disorder: Embracing disorganization at home and in the workplace.* Grass Valley, CA: Underwood Books.

Svantesson, I. (1998). *Learning maps and memory skills* (2nd ed.). London, England: Kogan Page.

Zeer, D. & Klein, M. (Illustrator) (2000). *Office yoga: Simple stretches for busy people.* San Francisco, CA: Chronicle Books.

CHAPTER 4 Energy

Eden, D. & Feinstein, D. (1989). *Energy medicine.* New York: J. P. Tarcher.

Rinzler, C. A. (1999). *Nutrition for dummies.* Hoboken, NJ: For Dummies.

Young, R. & Young, S. R. (2000). *Sick and tired?: Reclaim your inner terrain.* Orem, UT: Woodland Publishing.

CHAPTER 5 Emotional Intelligence

Bar-On, R. & Parker, J. D. A. (Eds.) (2000). *The handbook of emotional intelligence: Theory, development, assessment, and application at home, school, and in the workplace.* San Francisco, CA: Jossey-Bass.

Cherniss, C. & Goleman, D. P. (Eds.) (2001). *The emotionally intelligent workplace: How to select for, measure, and improve emotional intelligence in individuals, groups, and organizations.* San Francisco, CA: Jossey-Bass.

Goleman, D. P. (1997). *Emotional intelligence.* New York: Bantam.

Goleman, D. P. (1997). *Working with emotional intelligence.* New York: Bantam.

Goleman, D. P., Boyatzis, R., & McKee, A. (2002). *Primal leadership: Realizing the power of emotional intelligence.* Cambridge, MA: Harvard Business School Press.

Lynn, A. B. (2001). *The emotional intelligence activity book: 50 activities for promoting EQ at work.* New York: AMACOM.

Naparstek, B. (1998). *Your sixth sense: Unlocking the power of your intuition.* New York: HarperCollins.

Pearsall, P. (1996). *The pleasure prescription: To love, to work, to play life in the balance.* Alameda, CA: Hunter House.

Seligman, M. E. (1998). *Learned optimism: How to change your mind and your life.* New York: Pocket Books.

Tansey, M. J. & Burke, W. F. (Contributor) (1995). *Understanding countertransference: From projective identification to empathy.* Hillsdale, NJ: Analytic Press.

Vaughan, S. C. (2001). *Half empty, half full: Understanding the psychological roots of optimism.* Ft. Washington, PA: Harvest Books.

Watzlawick, P., Weakland, J., & Fisch, R. (1988). *Change: Principles of problem formation and problem resolution.* New York: Norton.

Weisinger, H. (1998). *Emotional intelligence at work: The untapped edge for success.* San Francisco, CA: Jossey-Bass.

CHAPTER 6 Integrity

Goleman, D. P., McKee, A., & Boyatzis, R. E. (2002). *Primal leadership: Realizing the power of emotional intelligence.* Boston: Harvard Business School Press.

Kouzes, J. M. & Posner, B. Z. (2002). *The leadership challenge* (3rd ed.). San Francisco, CA: Jossey-Bass.

Maxwell, J. C. & Ziglar, Z. (1998). *The 21 irrefutable laws of leadership.* Nashville, TN: Thomas Nelson.

CHAPTER 7 Integration

Allen, D. (2003). *Getting things done: The art of stress-free productivity.* New York: Penguin.

Emmett, R. (2000). *The procrastinator's handbook: Mastering the art of doing it now.* New York: Walker & Co.

Lagatree, K. M. (2000). *Checklists for life: 104 lists to help you get organized, save time, and unclutter your life.* New York: Random House.

Morgenstern, J. (2000). *Time management from the inside out: The foolproof system for taking control of your schedule and your life.* New York: Henry Holt.

Tracy, B. (2001). *Eat that frog!: 21 great ways to stop procrastinating and get more done in less time.* San Francisco, CA: Berrett-Koehler.

Index